Children of the
Cultural Revolution

Children of the Cultural Revolution

Family Life and Political Behavior in Mao's China

Xiaowei Zang

A Member of the Perseus Books Group

Copyright © 2000 by Westview Press, A Member of the Perseus Books Group

Published in 2000 in the United States of America by Westview Press, 5500 Central Avenue, Boulder, Colorado 80301-2877, and in the United Kingdom by Westview Press, 12 Hid's Copse Road, Cumnor Hill, Oxford OX2 9JJ

Find us on the World Wide Web at www.westviewpress.com

Library of Congress Cataloging-in-Publication Data
Zang, Xiaowei.
   Children of the cultural revolution : family life and political behavior in Mao's China / by Xiaowei Zang.
      p.   cm.
   Includes bibliographical references and index.
   ISBN 0-8133-3731-3 (hc)
   1. Family—China. 2. Social classes—China. 3. Caste—China. 4. Political participation—China. 5. China—History—Cultural Revolution, 1966–1976. I. Title.

HQ648.Z35   1999
306.85'0951—dc21   99-045378

10   9   8   7   6   5   4   3   2   1

This book is dedicated to the Children of the Cultural Revolution.

Contents

Tables

Acknowledgments

After I finished my dissertation on class and political behavior in Mao's China at Berkeley in 1992, I became preoccupied with different research interests. Nevertheless, I have never hesitated to spend time on converting my dissertation into book form. This has meant a lot to me because it has kept alive my memory of the six years my family and I spent in the San Francisco Bay Area. My wife, Yuling, sacrificed her academic ambition to support our children during our stay in Albany, California. She never failed to urge me to be all I could be. Without her encouragement, I probably would not be where I am today. I want to thank her from the bottom of my heart. I also want to extend thanks to my daughter, Lisa, and my son, Lucien. They have taught me to be a better person and have filled my life with beautiful sunshine.

While I acknowledge full responsibility for this work and any errors it may contain, many people have been generous with their time in helping me complete my project. Foremost is my dissertation committee at Berkeley, Thomas Gold, Michael Hout, and Elizabeth Perry. Their expert counsel and comments were invaluable. Elizabeth Perry has encouraged me to publish my dissertation since 1992. So have Thomas Gold, Michael Hout, and Graeme Lang, my colleague at City University of Hong Kong. Andrew Walder read my dissertation and gave many valuable suggestions. I also benefited from comments on my job talk from my former colleagues in the Department of Sociology at the Flinders University of South Australia. I am, however, solely responsible for the interpretations and materials presented in this book.

I would also like to thank Samuel Gaylord for his editorial assistance in preparing this book.

The Institute of International Studies at University of California at Berkeley provided partial financial support for my field research in the form of a Simpson Dissertation Fellowship for the academic year of 1990-1991.

This book is based on my interviews with fifty-seven Chinese students and immigrants in the San Francisco Bay Area between 1990 and 1991. I wish to thank them wholeheartedly. They generously shared their personal stories with me. Their Cultural Revolution experience helped shape my approach toward the study of family life and behavioral development in China.

Writing this book was a self-rediscovery process. Before my field research, I had sometimes unconsciously and at other times consciously allowed myself to forget my own Cultural Revolution experience. The Cultural Revolution seemed remote from my personal life when I chose in 1990 to study how it had desocialized Chinese youth. My informants' stories led me to relive the stressful period of the Cultural Revolution and helped me realize my obligation as a victim of that traumatic era **never to forget the Cultural Revolution**. Their stories accompanied me throughout this project and made it a very moving and unforgettable experience for me.

Xiaowei Zang
Hong Kong

1

INTRODUCTION

Children of the Cultural Revolution refers to the Red Guard generation, children who were in China's primary and secondary schools at the outset of the Cultural Revolution in 1966. Many Western scholars have studied the Red Guard generation.[1] I draw insights from their writings to develop new understanding and a fresh perspective on family life and behavioral development before and during the Cultural Revolution. I also seek to discover and analyze the factors that influence political behavior in China in general.

To help readers better appreciate what I aim to achieve in this book, it is necessary that I explain a few important concepts and my methodology.

The Cultural Revolution

The term, *Cultural Revolution*, is commonly used to refer to the 1966-1976 decade of relentless social upheaval in the People's Republic of China. In essence, the Cultural Revolution was a result of the power struggle between Mao Zedong, Chairman of the Chinese Communist Party (hereafter the CCP), and Liu Shaoqi, President of the People's Republic of China. It arose from their different concepts of culture and art, educational reforms, economic policies, the nature of political institutions and, ultimately, what each saw as the proper road to socialism in China.[2]

Mao was angered by prevailing bourgeois attitudes in the sciences and culture and by persistent inequality in income and prestige between mental and manual labor, between rural and urban areas, and between workers and peasants. What alarmed him most, however, was his belief that Liu Shaoqi and his followers had formed a bourgeois dictatorship, controlling the masses in state enterprises, public hospitals, schools, research institutes and other government organizations.[3]

In 1966 Mao plotted to oust Liu from the power circle. Liu, however, was firmly supported by many CCP leaders and government officials. Mao thus decided to dismantle the CCP system and the government hierarchy in order to "purify" the bureaucracy. Making certain that the People's Liberation Army (hereafter the PLA) endorsed his plan, Mao then called on the youth of China to launch the Cultural Revolution. He declared that it was justifiable to rebel against all sorts of authority in China. Millions of students responded to his call, forming Red Guard detachments in a concerted attack on leading writers, school teachers, "bad elements" (erstwhile landlords, rich peasants, capitalists, rightists, and former officials of the pre-1949 Nationalist government) and other "reactionaries".[4]

In the strife that followed, many middle class professionals and government officials were placed on the hit list of the Red Guards. Social turmoil followed as all controlling agencies (except the PLA) broke down. To restore social order, Mao was led to grant sweeping power to the PLA. This failed to halt a nationwide seesawing clash between "radicals" led by Jiang Qing, Mao's wife, and "conservatives" represented by Zhou Enlai, China's Premier at the time, and Deng Xiaoping. The Cultural Revolution officially came to a close with the death of Mao and the subsequent arrest of Jiang Qing and her associates in 1976.[5]

The Cultural Revolution had disastrous impact on Chinese society.[6] Chinese officials have maintained that about one hundred million people (or more than one-tenth of the country's population at the time) suffered during the Cultural Revolution.[7] Some people believe that Red Guard violence led to the death of twenty million people. A much lower estimate of the fatalities numbers the deaths at one million.[8] Labor productivity suffered, so did people's earning power.[9] The Cultural Revolution disrupted the life course of millions of urban youth. Between 1968 and 1975, approximately twenty million young people were forced by the government to leave cities and settle down in rural areas. This was perhaps one of the largest human migrations in history.[10]

Because of its tragic nature and destructive magnitude, the Cultural Revolution has been an important subject of Chinese studies.[11] Crises such as the Cultural Revolution reveal the inner workings and problematic features of social life in a significant way. As Glen H. Elder points out, shifts in power and allegiance that in a peaceful period may take years to occur, develop suddenly in a few weeks, days or hours in a crisis situation.[12] Instances of such situations thus offer researchers unique opportunities to observe and interpret the social structures that affect rapid social change. The Cultural Revolution provides a background for a good understanding of the determinants underlying political behavior in China.

Methodological Approach

More than twenty-three years have passed since the Cultural Revolution ended in 1976. Nevertheless, we have not accumulated sufficient knowledge about family life and political behavior and the linkage between these two aspects of social life during the period of upheaval. It is widely believed that during the traumatic period of 1966-1976 almost the entire population was victimized and virtually every adolescent was a Red Guard. Most existing scholarship dealing with the Cultural Revolution focuses on former Red Guards and on those among the intellectual elite victimized by the social disorder.[13]

However, little is known about family life and political behavior of ordinary Chinese who were neither among the Red Guards nor political victims of the Cultural Revolution. They were the "silent majority". Their stories may more accurately reflect Chinese society than the accounts of highly placed Chinese intellectuals with privileged access to Western academics with whom they are eager to share their traumatic experience. The Cultural Revolution experience of ordinary Chinese differs from that of the intellectual elite and even among themselves there was great variation in family life and political participation during the period.

It is this variation and factors producing it that comprise the central theme of this book. On the basis of my interviews with children of the Cultural Revolution, I argue that life styles and political orientations varied among Chinese families of different socioeconomic status before 1966. These families traveled on different life paths during the Cultural Revolution. The differences in family socioeconomic status were related 1) to the variations in the meanings of the Cultural Revolution and 2) to the potential for adapting to or coping with the upheaval, and thus to the linkages between family background and behavior patterns.[14]

This line of analysis rests on the assumption that social being determines social consciousness which in turn influences behavior. C. Wright Mills argues that the life stories of men and women, the kinds of individuals they have become, cannot be understood without reference to the historical milieu in which their everyday lives are patterned and organized. Historical transformations carry meanings not only for individual ways of life, but for the very character, the limits and possibilities of human experience.[15]

Existing Theoretical Frameworks on Political Behavior in China

This focus on family socioeconomic status differs from three sociological approaches to understanding political behavior in China: 1) a traditional political culture model; 2) a communist clientelist paradigm; and 3) a family political status perspective.

Traditional Political Culture

The traditional political culture model holds that a deep understanding of Chinese politics requires a similar understanding of China's traditional political culture. Political beliefs and norms inherited from the past provide controlling guidelines for behavior in China. Important themes in Chinese political tradition include the version of a rigidly defined order of role relationships, etiquette, ritual, obedience, dependence on authority figures, repression of aggression, collectivity, and the paramount value of filial piety.[16]

The political culture model has been criticized for its cultural determinism since the 1970s. Nevertheless, some scholars have refused to rule out its usefulness in the study of Chinese political behavior.[17]

Communist Clientelism

Communist clientelism proposes that political authority and stability are largely maintained through patron-client synergy, i.e., clients in exchange for political support are rewarded with preferential treatment by patrons. The rewards include career opportunities, housing, special distributions, and other benefits monopolized by the CCP officials. The exchange generates a stable patron-client relationship between the CCP cadres and their followers.[18]

For example, in factories some workers became political activists in order to obtain CCP membership, housing, promotions and other social benefits.[19] In rural areas some peasants, in order to maximize their material interests, became clients of production team leaders.[20] In schools some students were politically active, accumulating political credentials that gained them eligibility for job or education opportunities. There was a social division between political activists and non-activists. Political behavior was regulated by the CCP's reward system.[21]

Family Political Status

The family political status model explains political behavior in Mao's China on the basis of a caste-like system. Many Western scholars observe that after 1949, the CCP classified Chinese people as "bad class", "middle class", or "good class", depending on their relationship to the means of production and to the pre-1949 Nationalist government. These three "classes" constituted a family political status system under Mao's rule (see Chapter 2).

These scholars view the family political status system as a quasi-caste system, with the "good class" comprising the upper caste and the "bad class" the lower caste. The "middle class", as its name suggests, is placed in the middle of the caste hierarchy and is not defined by its economic resources.

These scholars have also noted that in addition to the "good class" and "bad class" there were occupational groups: workers, cadres, intellectuals including university professors and writers, professionals such as doctors, engineers, and others. Often, occupational groups are incorporated into the family political status system. For example, workers and cadres are viewed as part of the "good class" and intellectuals as part of the "middle class".[22] Being the most important factor of social stratification, family political status influenced family life and political behavior in Mao's China.[23]

A Family Socioeconomic Status Approach

In this book I seek, on the basis of existing studies, to develop a family socioeconomic approach to understanding life chances and behavioral development in China. I am inspired by Glen H. Elder's argument that a specific stimulus condition in a historical period tends to vary in its effect on different population subsets, defined by class, sex, etc.[24] Since the Cultural Revolution was an anti-establishment social movement, I reasons that it was highly likely that Chinese working class families reached higher rungs of the prestige ladder. However, their resources for coping with material shortage remained inadequate.

In comparison, middle class families might worry more about status or loss of reputation than about daily necessities. In a crisis situation such as given rise by the Cultural Revolution, families of the middle and lower classes faced different problems, commanded different resources for dealing with the new situation, and relied on a variety of means by which to adapt.

Therefore, there is a strong possibility that the pre-1966 family socioeconomic status led to variations in the problems, the potential, and the patterns of adaptation among Chinese families during the period of upheaval. E. P. Thompson reminds us that if we freeze history at any particular moment, there will be no social context at all, other than a multitude of unconnected individuals. But as soon as individuals acquire a past and future, it becomes clear from the recurrent patterns in their life paths that they interact through group process.[25]

Accordingly, I start my inquiry with the observation that the social structure in Mao's China consisted of a family political status system (Chapter 2) and a class hierarchy based on a job ranking system (Chapter 3).[26] The socioeconomic status of each family was jointly determined by its family political status and class position. I investigate daily life and behavior patterns by looking simultaneously at the family political status system and socioeconomic hierarchy under Mao.

Despite my emphasis on the linkage between political behavior and family socioeconomic status, I incorporate in this book the notion of the traditional political culture model wherein norms and values have an impact on behavior. Nevertheless, I argue that there are variations in norms and values among people of different socioeconomic status. In fact, many sociologists have long recognized that upper class people adhere to high culture; and lower class people, low culture. Families of different socioeconomic status exhibit different patterns of behavior partly because of their different value systems. I thus view values and norms as an intervening variable between political behavior, the dependent variable; and family socioeconomic status, the independent variable.

I similarly take into account the notion of communist clientelism that political behavior revolves around the reward system controlled by the CCP. I nevertheless stress that individuals of different socioeconomic status respond to the opportunity structure in a variety of ways. They receive different education and political socialization due to different levels of access to financial resources.[27] Middle class people are more likely than those of the lower class to have high motivations to respond to the opportunity structure. In the final analysis, it is family socioeconomic status, rather than the opportunity structure, that determines political behavior in China.

I also agree that the family political status system was an important dimension of stratification in Mao's China. In fact, the family socioeconomic status approach I propose in this book owes its origin to the family political status model. Nevertheless, I write this book with a firm belief that an exclusive attention on the political status differences between the "good class" and "bad class" in instrumental and expressive capacities may not lead to an accurate description of social life in Mao's China. Students of the family political status model have examined political activism among some members of the "good class" in great detail but have paid scant attention to political inaction among others in the same group. They also fail to observe the variations in behavioural patterns among members of the lower caste.

I also notice that some students of the family political status model rely on occupational group association (i.e., workers, cadres, intellectuals, etc.) to explain political behavior. In this work, I use socioeconomic differences within each occupational group to analyze their impact on family life and behavioral patterns. I emphasize the socioeconomic reality and do not regard occupational groups as the basic element of the social structure in Mao's China. Inequality in income and prestige within each occupational group significantly reduces the occupational group coherence and diverts political activity and individual allegiances from occupational group identifications.

Further, I realize that I rely on stratification for an understanding of the linkage between social status differences and political behavior as students of the family political status model do. However, their stratification scheme is based on the family political status system, whereas mine revolves around the family political status system and occupational ranking hierarchy. This difference in categorization has helped me unearth new evidence concerning family life and political behavior in Mao's China.

Finally, scholars of the family political status system are interested in studying the relationship between caste groups and Red Guard factionalism during the Cultural Revolution.[28] I am certainly interested in this linkage. My main concern in this work however is to explain different life experiences and patterns of political participation among various social status groups within each caste. These are important issues that have not been explored adequately by the family political status system model.

Concepts in the Analytic Framework

To study social life under Mao, I follow the analytic framework presented in *Children of the Great Depression* by Glen H. Elder.[29] I rely heavily on four concepts, class, caste, adaptation, and subgroup, to assess and interpret the effects of family socioeconomic status on life styles and behavior patterns.

Class

The concept of class is the analytical foundation of this book. Class can be conceptualized in more than one way. In this book I define it in terms of income, occupational prestige and social status. These three elements comprise an important dimension of social stratification[30] with profound impact on political behavior. Classes defined as such should be understood as strata. Like most American scholars, I take the liberty of substituting classes for strata.

In the following analysis, the concept of class appears in the form of some basic questions about the nature of social relations and interactions before and during the Cultural Revolution. What were the links between socioeconomic status and political behavior? What was the interplay between values and the social hierarchy in Mao's China?

The class approach can provide a good explanatory framework allowing us to subdue the chaos of individual experience and to illustrate the social experience of people in groups over time. Alan Dawley states that a strong appeal of class analysis is its capacity to encompass a rich variety of materials from a broad range of human experience—social, economic, and political. If various materials are thought of as the flakes of brightly colored stone in the barrel of a kaleidoscope, then class relations are the maroons that impart patterns to the stone flakes.[31]

Caste

According to the family political status model, the "good class", "bad class" and "middle class" in Mao's China functioned as castes. Strictly speaking, they were not true castes since they were not based on occupations as in India. Nevertheless, I agree with students of the family political status model that these "classes" can be viewed as castes because they resembled the Indian counterparts in that the "class" labels were inheritable and were an important determinant for employment, education and marriage.

Many scholars adopt the Chinese usage of "good class" and "bad class" to describe the caste system in the Mao era. I follow the conventional categorization of castes in this book. Upper caste and "good class" are used here interchangeably. So are the lower caste and "bad class" (see Chapter 2). These were political status groups and should not be confused with the use of upper, middle, and lower class in the following analysis. There the reference is to socioeconomic status groups (see Chapter 3). In the following seven chapters I study how class and caste were mutually related and how this influenced family life and political behavior in the Mao era.

Crisis and Adaptation

To numerous Chinese families and China experts, the Cultural Revolution was a crisis. As Glen H. Elder points out, a crisis refers to a problematic disparity between the claims of a family in a situation and its control of outcomes or, more specifically, to a gap between socioeconomic needs and the ability to satisfy them. Crises challenge customary interpretations of reality and undermine established psychological equilibrium. The disruption of habitual ways of life produces new stimuli that elicit attention and arouse consciousness of self and others.[32]

Adaptation involves a redefinition of self and others, the clarification of life goals, and struggles to achieve control over outcomes and to reach a new psychological equilibrium. The basic features of this approach are attributable to the work of Glen H. Elder, *Children of the Great Depression*, which was written under the influence of *The Polish Peasant in Europe and America (1918-20)* by William Isaac Thomas and Florian Znaniecke.[33]

According to Glen H. Elder, crises and lines of adaptation emerge when individuals or groups interact with situations. A problematic disparity between claims and control activates consciousness, attention capacities, and methods of problem solving in the construction of new forms of adaptation. Two sets of individual characteristics bear upon the adaptation process: 1) claims or expectations with respect to outcomes, and 2) modes of adaptive potential. Both result from family resources and family socialization. Adaptive potential includes a positive image of self, problem-solving skills, a sense of confidence and competence, incentives for engaging in productive behavior, and the mechanisms an individual employs to reach his or her goals.[34]

Adaptive potential not only refers to an individual's goals (the motivation), but also to the resources he or she can mobilize in dealing with particular challenges. From a developmental perspective, we can trace an individual's coping abilities and motivation to his or her past family experience.[35] Glen H. Elder's approach assumes that there are social status differences in society that give people different attitudes and political orientations during a crisis. I build my arguments on the basis of his insights to study political behavior of the children of the Cultural Revolution.

Subgroup Comparison

Subgroup distinctions enter into the assessment of the variations in family life and political behavior in Mao's China. Subgroups are created by dividing Chinese families within each political status category (i.e., the "good class" and "bad class") into different socioeconomic status groups. Chapter 3 shows that there were three classes, upper, middle and lower, within each caste. Subgroups are then compared with one another to provide an understanding of how each was associated with a particular set of life experience, opportunities and resources and how this bore upon the derivational experience of families and individuals in Mao' China.

Specifically, I structure the following analysis around four groups of parents and children as defined by class and caste. Within the middle class and lower class, I compare the life experience and personality of persons who grew up in the upper caste and lower caste families respectively.

Organization of the Book

I organize this book both chronologically and comparatively. Chapters 2, 3, and 4 provide the necessary historical background relating to the formation of social classes and the caste system (i.e., the family political status system) in Mao's China. These three chapters offer no new evidence on social stratification prior to the Cultural Revolution. However, most of the findings on stratification in pre-1966 China were published in Chinese only.

More importantly, these three chapters combine existing scholarly arguments on social inequality in China to create a new stratification scheme for classifying Chinese people into various groups, which allows readers to understand Mao's China from a new perspective.

Chapter 5 discusses the variations in family life and behavior patterns among families of different socioeconomic status in the pre-1966 Chinese society, analyzing patterns of consumption, values, expectations, and political participation. This chapter supplies a historical context needed for the understanding of subsequent events. The effects of the variation in family life and behavior patterns are then traced in the later chapters to the variations in adaptation problems, adaptation resources, and adaptation patterns among families of different socioeconomic status during the Cultural Revolution.

Chapter 6 studies the personal experience of children in the upper caste middle class during the Cultural Revolution. It discusses the social dislocation among middle class families and how family deprivation served as a stimulus for upper caste middle class children to search for adaptive strategies to reclaim lost status.

Chapter 7 investigates family life and political behavior of children of the upper caste lower class during the same historical period, focusing on their daily concerns and political inaction during the Cultural Revolution. Chapters 6 and 7 may be read as one unit to understand the differences in behavior between children of the upper caste middle class and their lower class counterparts.

Chapter 8 examines the life paths of the lower caste middle class and lower caste lower class during the Cultural Revolution, illustrating how the differences in family resources and the pre-1966 socialization experience of these two groups led them to adopt different strategies for dealing with the stressful situation.

Chapter 9 summarizes the major findings of this book and discusses the socioeconomic development and changing patterns of stratification in post-Mao China. It also examines the linkage between socioeconomic status and political behavior in the post-Mao era. This chapter concludes the book by suggesting that class analysis can be productively applied to the study of contemporary Chinese politics.

I seek in this book to use class analysis to link political behavior with family socioeconomic status and to describe selected aspects of social institutions and behavioral patterns in Mao's China. I hope that this book will be part of the exploratory work of social science out of which more authoritative descriptions of reality in China will emerge. Readers who are interested in the methodological issues should refer to Appendix I at the end of this book.

Notes

1. Anita Chan, Richard Madsen, and Jonathan Unger, "Students and Class Warfare: the Social Roots of the Red Guard Conflict in Guangzhou (Canton)." *The China Quarterly* (September 1980) 80: Pp. 397-446; Julia Kwong, *The Cultural Revolution in China's School* (Stanford: Hoover Institution Press, 1988); Hong Yung Lee, *The Politics of the Cultural Revolution* (Berkeley: University of California Press, 1978); Jing Lin, *The Red Guards' Path to Violence: Political, Educational, and Psychological Factors* (New York: Praeger, 1991); Stanley Rosen, *Red Guard Factionalism and the Cultural Revolution in Guangzhou* (Boulder: Westview Press, 1982); Susan Shirk, *Competitive Comrades* (Berkeley: University of California Press, 1982); Richard Solomon, *Mao's Revolution and the Chinese Political Culture* (Berkeley: University of California Press, 1972); Gordon White, *The Politics of Class and Class Origins* (Contemporary China Centre, The Australian National University, 1974).

2. Barbara Barnouin and Yu Changgen (eds.) *Ten Years of Turbulence* (London and New York: Kegan Paul International, 1993); Lowell Dittmer, *Liu Shao-chi and the Chinese Cultural Revolution* (Berkeley: University of California Press, 1974); Harry Harding, *Organizing China* (Stanford: Stanford University Press, 1981); Shaorong Huang, *To Rebel Is Justified: A Rhetorical Study of China's Cultural Revolution Movement 1966-1969* (Lanham: University Press of America, 1996); William A. Joseph, Christine Wong, and David Zweig (eds.) *New Perspectives on the Cultural Revolution* (Cambridge: Council on East Asian Studies, Harvard University, 1991); Roderick MacFarquhar, *Origins of the Cultural Revolution Vol. I* (New York: Columbia University Press, 1974); Suzanne Pepper, *Radicalism and Education in 20th-Century China* (New York: Cambridge University Press, 1996); Elizabeth J. Perry and Li Xun (eds.) *Proletarian Power: Shanghai in the Cultural Revolution* (Boulder: Westview Press, 1997); Michael Schoenhals (ed.) *China's Cultural Revolution 1966-1969* (Armonk: M. E. Sharpe, 1996); Wang Shaoguang, *Failure of Charisma: The Cultural Revolution in Wuhan* (Hong Kong: Oxford University Press, 1995); Lynn White, *Politics of Chaos* (Princeton: Princeton Press, 1989); Yen Chia-chi and Kao Kao, *The Ten-Year History of the Chinese Cultural Revolution* (Taiwan: Institute of Current China Studies, 1988).

3. Dittmer 1974 (footnote 2); Harding 1981 (footnote 2); Kwong 1988 (footnote 1); Pepper 1996 (footnote 2); Yen and Kao 1988 (footnote 2).

4. Michael Frolic, *Mao's People* (Cambridge: Harvard University Press, 1980); Harding 1981 (footnote 2); Kwong 1988 (footnote 1); Lin 1991 (footnote 1); Richard Madsen, "The Politics of Revenge in Rural China during the Cultural Revolution." Pp. 175-202 in Jonathan Lipman and Steven Harrell (eds.) *Violence in China* (Albany: State University of New York Press, 1990); Anne F. Thurston, *Enemies of the People* (New York: Knopf, 1987); Yen and Kao 1988 (footnote 2).

5. Yen and Kao 1988 (footnote 2). Some scholars argue that the Cultural Revolution ended in 1969, see Kwong 1988 (footnote 1) and White 1989 (footnote 2).

6. Frolic 1980 (footnote 4); Fulang Lo, *Morning Breeze* (San Francisco: China Books & Periodicals, 1989); Lu Xinhua et al., (Gerenie Barme and Bennet Lee, trans.) *The Wounded* (Hong Kong: Joint Publishing Company, 1979); Helen Siu and Zelda Stern (eds.) *Mao's Harvest* (New York: Oxford University Press, 1983); Thurston 1987 (footnote 4); White 1989 (footnote 2); Yen and Kao 1988 (footnote 2).

7. Andrew Nathan, *Chinese Democracy* (Berkeley: University of California Press, 1986), p. 5.

8. White 1989 (footnote 2), p. 7; Anne Thurston, "Urban Violence During the Cultural Revolution." Pp. 149-174 in Lipman and Harrell 1990 (footnote 4).

9. Robert Michael Field, "Slow Growth of Labor Productivity in Chinese Industry, 1951-1981." *The China Quarterly* (December 1983) 96: Pp. 647-650; Andrew Walder, "Wage Reform and the Web of Factory Interest." *The China Quarterly* (December 1987) 109: Pp. 22-41.

10. For more information on this event, see Thomas Bernstein, *Up to the Mountain and Down to the Village* (New Haven: Yale University Press, 1977); Deng Xian, *Zhongguo Zhiqing Meng* (The Dream of the Educated Youth in China) (Beijing: Renmin Wenxue Chubanshe, 1993); Thomas Gold, "State and Youth." *The China Quarterly* (December 1991) 127: Pp. 594-612; Peter Seybolt, *The Rustication of Urban Youth in China* (New York; M. E. Sharpe, 1977); Xueguang Zhou and Liren Hou, "Children of the Cultural Revolution: The State and the Life Course in the People's Republic of China." *American Sociological Review* (1999) 64/1: Pp. 12-36.

11. See footnotes 1& 2 for representative works on the Cultural Revolution.

12. Glen H. Elder, *Children of the Great Depression* (Chicago: University of Chicago Press, 1974).

13. Chan, Madsen, and Unger 1982 (footnote 1); Frolic 1980 (footnote 4); Lin 1991 (footnote 1); Lu 1979 (footnote 6); Rosen 1982 (footnote 1); Shirk 1982 (footnote 1); Siu and Stern 1983 (footnote 6); Solomon 1972 (footnote 1); Thurston 1987 (footnote 4); Thurston 1990 (footnote 8); White 1974 (footnote 1).

14. This line of analysis is indebted to Elder 1974 (footnote 12).

15. C. Wright Mills, *The Sociological Imagination* (New York: Oxford University Press, 1959).

16. See Lucian. W. Pye and Sidney Verba (eds*.) Political Culture and Political Development* (Princeton: Princeton University Press, 1965); Lucian W. Pye, *The Spirit of Chinese Politics* (Cambridge: Oelgeschlager, Gunn & Hain, 1981); Lucian W. Pye, *Asian Power and Politics* (Cambridge: The Belnap Press, 1985); Lucian W. Pye, *The Mandarin and the Cadre* (Ann Arbor: Center for Chinese Studies, University of Michigan, 1988); Solomon 1972 (footnote 1). Also see Xiaowei Zang, *Children of the Cultural Revolution: Class and Caste in Mao's China* (Ph.D. dissertation, University of California, Berkeley, 1992), Chapter 2.

17. Lucian W. Pye, "The Escalation of Confrontation." Pp. 162-179 in George Hicks (ed.) *The Broken Mirror* (Chicago: St. James Press, 1990); Jeffrey N. Wasserstrom and Elizabeth J. Perry (eds.) *Popular Protest and Political Culture in Modern China* (Boulder: Westview, 1992).

18. Jean Oi, "Communism and Clientelism." *World Politics* (1985) 3/2: Pp. 328-366; Shirk 1982 (footnote 1); Andrew Walder, *Communist Neo-Traditionalism* (Berkeley: University of California Press, 1986); also see Christopher Clapham (ed.) *Private Patronage and Public Power, Political Clientelism in the Modern State* (London: Frances Pinter, 1982); Shmuel Noah Eisenstadt and Gene Lemarchand, (eds.) *Political Clientelism, Patronage and Development* (Berveley Hill: Sage Publications, 1981); Thomas Henry Rigby, "The Need for Comparative Research on Clientelism." *Studies in Comparative Communism* (Summer/Autumn 1979) 12: Pp. 204-211; Thomas Henry Rigby, *Leadership Selection and Patron-Client Relations in the USSR and Yugoslavia* (London: Allen & Unwind, 1983); John Willerton, "Clientelism in the Soviet Union." *Studies in Comparative Communism* (Summer/Autume 1979) 12: Pp. 159-211; Zang 1992 (footnote 16).

19. Walder 1986 (footnote 18).

20. Oi 1985 (footnote 18).

21. Shirk 1982 (footnote 1).

22. Chan, Madsen, and Unger 1980 (footnote 1); Lee 1978 (footnote 1); Rosen 1982 (footnote 1); White 1974 (footnote 1).

23. Elizabeth Croll, *The Politics of Marriage in Contemporary China* (Cambridge: Cambridge University Press, 1981); Richard Kraus, *Class Conflict in Chinese Socialism* (New York: Columbia University Press, 1981); Lee 1978 (footnote 1); Rosen 1982 (footnote 1); White 1974 (footnote 1); White 1989 (footnote 2), Pp. 87-90. Also see Zang 1992 (footnote 16), Chapter 2.

24. Elder 1974 (footnote 12).

25. E. P. Thompson, *The Making of the English Working Class* (New York: Vintage Books, 1966), p. 11 & Preface.

26. Kraus 1981 (footnote 23).

27. Alan Grey, *Class and Personality in Society* (New York: Atherton Press, 1969).

28. See Chan, Madsen, and Unger 1982 (footnote 1); Rosen 1982 (footnote 1).

29. Elder 1974 (footnote 12).

30. Some China experts have devised a list of eight separate dimensions of inequality. See Martin King Whyte, "Social Trends in China." Pp. 103-123 in A. Doak Barnett and Ralph N. Clough (eds.) *Modernizing China* (Boulder: Westview Press, 1986).

31. Reinhard Bendix and Seymour Martin Lipset (eds.) *Class, Statues and Power* (Glencoe: The Free Press, 1953); Alan Dawley, *Class and Community* (Cambridge: Harvard University Press, 1979), p. 4.

32. Elder 1974 (footnote 12); Glen H. Elder, "Perspectives on the Life Course." Pp. 23-49 in Glen H. Elder (ed.) *Life Course Dynamics: Trajectories and Transitions, 1968-1980* (Ithaca: Cornell University Press, 1985); Glen H. Elder, "The Life Course Paradigm: Social Change and Individual Development." Pp. 101-139 in Phyllis Moen, Glen H. Elder, and Kurt Luscher (eds.) *Examining Lives in Context* (Washington DC: American Psychological Association, 1995); Linda K. George, "Sociological Perspective on Life Transitions." *Annual Review of Sociology* (1993) 19: Pp. 353-373.

33. William Isaac Thomas and Florian Znaniecke, *The Polish Peasant in Europe and America (1918-20)* (Urbana: University of Illinois Press, 1984).

34. Elder 1974 (footnote 12).

35. Elder 1974 (footnote 12).

2

THE POLITICAL STATUS SYSTEM

After twenty-eight years of armed struggle, the CCP finally came to power in 1949. Its victory reshaped social relationships in China. Before 1949, social stratification was based mainly on private ownership and occupational grouping. There were property-based classes: a working class, a capitalist class, landlords, etc. and occupation-based strata: middle class professionals, etc.

After the nationalization of the means of production in the 1950s, political status replaced private ownership as a stratifying element. At the same time, occupational ranking emerged as another important factor contributing to social inequality in Mao's China (see Chapter 3). Associated with these post-1949 patterns of social stratification were two important social hierarchies: a caste system based on the pre-1949 class relationships and a class structure based on the post-1949 occupational ranking.[1]

The caste hierarchy (i.e., the political status system) had a strong historical root. In this chapter, I first briefly discuss social stratification in the Qing Dynasty (1640-1911) and the Republic era of 1912-1949. Next, I review two studies of social stratification and class formation prior to the founding of the People's Republic of China in 1949. I pay particular attention to Mao Zedong's analysis of social classes in the 1920s. Mao's idea of class formation was practised after 1949 and had great influence on the formation of the family political status system. My discussion of this system is not a lengthy one since it has been a subject of intensive research since the 1970s. I will discuss the post-1949 class structure in Chapter 3.

Social Stratification in Ancient Regime

In imperial China, the state divided the population into four official social strata: scholar-officials, peasants, artisans and merchants. The strata were defined primarily on the basis of occupations rather than ownership of the means of production.[2] Therefore, the categorization did not reflect occupational reality and social inequality accurately.

For example, the category of peasantry included landless peasants, small farmers, big landlords and gentry, although they differed greatly from one another in terms of wealth and political power.

China's population approximated four hundred million around 1800. Among them, less than 5 million made their living by handicraft or trade in urban areas. Affluent merchants and gentry numbered 1.5 million and 1.1 million respectively. The rest were landlords, small farmers and landless peasants.[3]

Intellectuals who had passed state examinations on Confucianism and held government posts were classified as scholar-officials. When they retired they became gentry—rich landlords with political influence on local affairs and high prestige in their communities.[4]

In the late nineteenth century, the average annual income of scholar-officials was 200 silver taels, which was thirteen times higher than that of manual workers (farmers, blacksmiths, etc.). The actual disparity should be even higher since this estimate did not include embezzlements and briberies that scholar-officials enjoyed.[5] A popular saying at the time was that a county magistrate (the lowest ranking government official) who had taken briberies much less than his greedy colleagues could make at least 100,000 silver taels in three years.

Therefore, in imperial China, an effective channel of upward mobility was to pass government examinations on Confucianism to become an official. In theory, imperial China was a relatively open society as there were virtually no formal eligibility restrictions for taking the examinations.

However, many peasants did not take the examinations because they could not afford time and tuition fees to prepare for the examinations. The examinations were difficult and the preparation process was necessarily a lengthy one. Wealth was a pre-requisite for one or his son(s) to learn Confucianism for passing the examinations. Thus, most scholars were from landlord families.[6]

Although late imperial China did not have a strong tradition of caste or caste-like structures,[7] pariah groups did exist. They were permanently banned from taking the examinations. People in this category (such as boat people and entertainers) were deemed to be unfit even to socialize with ordinary Chinese. They were social isolates, outside the fabric of respectable community life. Their pariah standing was upheld by imperial dicta rather than by popular sentiment.[8] At some points in time pariah groups represented one percent of the population. In the middle Qing Dynasty there were no social pariah groups except boat people.[9]

In general, people became pariah either because of their occupations (entertainment, etc.), or because of political prosecutions. Losers of power struggles and their children, if not beheaded, were made entertainers or slaves of the state. Sometimes the losers' relatives were also made social pariah. I show in the following that Mao's regime similarly turned losers of political struggles into social pariah.

Social Stratification during the Republic Era

The Opium War of 1840-1842 marked the beginning of the large-scale Western penetration into Chinese society. Trade between China and the West had existed before the war and increased greatly after 1842.[10] Along China's coastline, major trade cities were established and prospered.[11] It was estimated that between 1840 and 1893, China's urban population swelled from 20 to 23.5 million. In other words, during this period, the proportion represented by urban residents rose from 5.1 to 6 percent of the total population.[12]

At the same time, there emerged modern social groups in China's coastal areas: industrial workers, professionals, modern intellectuals, industrialists, and commercial capitalists.[13] The Qing Dynasty was overthrown by a bourgeois revolution in 1911 and a Nationalist government ruled Mainland China between 1912 and 1949.

The period of 1912-1936 was the golden age of the Chinese bourgeoisie. The annual industrial growth rate in China during this period was 9.4 percent, as compared with 6.6 percent in Japan, 4.4 percent in the UK, and 7.9 percent in the USSR.[14] Marie-Claire Bergere estimates that by 1933 the Chinese factory production of cotton textiles amounted to about three-fourths of the Japanese total outcome. Aside from Japan, only the United States and India surpassed the scale of the Chinese cotton textile production. China's cotton consumption matched the combined total of Britain and Germany. The output of China's flour-mills exceeded Japanese results by a wide margin (1.66 : 1.05).[15]

However, industrialization was limited to a few light industries and failed to generate major changes in China's overall economic structure. China's nascent industries did not produce a substantial share of national economic activity. In 1933, for example, factory output stood for only 2.1 percent of the gross domestic production. Chinese producers in metallurgy, chemicals, and other basic industries did not attain significant quantitative dimensions in international terms.[16]

Thus, the modern working class numbered three million only in 1949. Agriculture was still the basis of China's economy. Over 85 percent of the population resided in rural areas and lived on farming. Landlords, who constituted only 10 percent of the total population, owned 70 percent of the land under cultivation. Most of the peasants were either renters or hired laborers working on landlords' farms.[17]

Studies of Social Stratification in the Pre-1949 Chinese Society

An important study of social stratification in the pre-1949 Chinese society is a 1926 monograph titled "An Analysis of the Classes in Chinese Society" by Mao Zedong.[18]

In the monograph Mao argued that there were six classes in China:

1. the landlord class and the comprador class;
2. the middle bourgeoisie;
3. the petty bourgeoisie, which included owner-peasants, master handicrafts-men, students, primary and secondary school-teachers, low government functionaries, office clerks, small lawyers and small traders;
4. peasants, the semi-proletariat, which included semi-owner peasants, poor handicraftsmen, shop assistants and peddlers;
5. the modern industrial proletariat;
6. the lumpen-proletariat.

Mao did not reject the concept of strata. He analyzed the strata within the petty bourgeoisie stratified by income. Noticeably, he did not categorize people on the basis of economic criteria alone. Political attitudes were an important factor to him in dividing the population into friends and enemies of the Communist Revolution. For example, he placed intellectuals holding negative attitudes toward the Chinese Communist Party into the category of the enemies of the people.[19]

Thus, Mao developed an economic and political attitude dimensions in his conceptualization of class formation. A person's "class" status was determined on the basis of his or her financial resources, or his or her political position, or the combination of both. Mao's ideas on stratification were put into practice in the post-1949 class labeling campaign.

Unlike Mao Zedong, American sociologist Olga Lang divided the Chinese population into three classes according to their income and prestige:[20]

1. the lower class, which included workers and small shop clerks in traditional occupations. Their wage range was from $2 to $15 a month.[21] The average monthly wage income for their families was $14.75; if other sources of income were included, it reached $16.90. Food was the biggest item on the budgets of such families. Their diet included mostly cereals and vegetables. Rice, meat, and fruit were eaten only on special occasions in connection with religious holidays. The living quarters for these families were overcrowded.[22]

   Workers in the modern sectors also belonged to the lower class. In 1937 the average monthly earning of Shanghai male workers was as follows: ship construction men, $40.92; printers, $36.17; machine workers, $26.00; flour-mill workers, $16.58; tobacco workers, $14.68; silk weavers, $18.66; cotton weavers, $15.84; and cotton spinners, $10.54. The average income of their families was $40.45 a month. Although cereals and vegetables were still the main items in their diet, meat and fish were found on their tables more frequently than those of workers in the traditional occupations. Their housing was not very good.[23]

2. the middle class, which included small merchants, owners of small workshops and factories, salaried employees, teachers of urban elementary and secondary schools, clerks, and junior civil and military officials. Their monthly income was from $30 to $120. Many of them owned land and had investments in factories and other businesses. They spent a smaller part of their income on food than the lower classes did. The quality of food and housing was better than that of the lower class.[24]
3. the upper class, which included high officials, leading intellectuals, big landlords and rich merchants. The salaries of high officials varied from $120 to $1,000 or more a month; the earnings of engineers in North China varied from $90 (beginners) to $360; in Shanghai, $500-$600; college professors in Beijing received $100-$600. Additionally, the upper class people had extra occupational sources of income (such as rent) which played a larger part in their economic life than in that of the middle class people.[25]

Other studies of social inequality in the Republic era (1912-1949) also show that during the 1930s, middle school teachers earned $100 per month; government officials with university education, $150 (briberies excluded); university teachers, engineers and technicians, $200; full professors, $300. A university graduate could make $100 per month after he or she worked more than one year.[26]

In contrast, the average monthly income of urban manual workers was below $15. Rural landless peasants earned even less. Workers and landless peasants comprised the vast majority of the population and were at the bottom of the socioeconomic hierarchy before 1949.[27]

Therefore, education continued to be a very important channel of upward mobility before the Sino-Japanese War of 1937-1945. The other two important avenues for upward mobility at the time were business and military service. A substantial proportion of new elites grew out of private business and the armed forces. They comprised the upper class and had great political power, wealth and influence.[28]

Intellectuals suffered greatly during the Sino-Japanese War. Their living standards improved during the period of 1946-1948. They experienced another devastating financial loss between 1948 and 1949. The Nationalist government relied on inflation to finance the Civil War against the CCP. Many middle class intellectuals and professionals could not even feed their families adequately. They thus participated in civil disobedience and anti-Nationalist government demonstrations.[29]

Other social groups also suffered financially during the Civil War of 1946-1949. Petty bourgeoisie, workers, clerks, peasants, and many others experienced inflationary spirals and were angered by the Nationalist government's fiscal policy. They gave their support to the CCP. This became an important reason for the CCP to come to power in 1949.[30]

The "Class" Labeling Campaign

The CCP was founded by a group of intellectuals in 1921 with the goal of creating a communist future for China and the world.[31] After the establishment of the People's Republic of China in 1949, the CCP began its campaign of socialist transformation. It theorized that the elimination of feudalism and capitalism was a precondition to the establishment of socialism in China. Feudalism, according to the CCP, was based on private land holding and represented by landlords and rich peasants. Between 1950 and 1952, the communist government sent land reform work teams to the countryside with the mission to destroy rural feudalism.[32]

The work teams first undertook a "class" labeling campaign to determine the targets of the land reforms. Rural residents were classified into the following categories: poor peasants, lower middle peasants, middle peasants, upper middle peasants, rich peasants and landlords. A person's "class" label was determined by the size of land he or she owned in 1949. The work teams sometimes arbitrarily assigned "class" labels to peasants. The total number of landlords and rich peasants in 1958 was estimated to be around 10,513,000.[33]

After the "class" labeling campaign, the work team confiscated properties from landlords and rich peasants for redistribution among poor and lower middle peasants. Landless peasants became small farmers.[34]

A similar process of "class" labeling was implemented in cities. In a series of political campaigns in the early 1950s, urban families were identified with labels such as capitalist, merchant, peddler, urban poor, clerk, staff, teacher, intellectual, worker and the like. The classification was based either on the pre-1949 ownership of the means of production or on occupations. Sometimes the classification was quite arbitrary since there were no precise official "class" definitions. Many small workshop owners and itinerant hawkers were labeled "capitalists".[35] According to one official estimate, over half a million individuals were identified as "capitalists" in 1956.[36] Another study claims that the number of "capitalists" was roughly 760,000. [37]

In addition to the "class" designations, there were negative political role labels assigned to the supporters and functionaries of the pre-1949 Nationalist government: reactionary despots, historical reactionaries, current reactionaries, and the like. Nearly four million people were categorized as the "bad elements".[38] After the 1957 Anti-Rightists Campaign,[39] half a million people, mostly intellectuals and government officials, were labeled "rightists" and were treated as the "bad elements".

Concurrent with the "class" labeling campaign, the government launched the socialist transformation movement. Between 1949 and 1952 land reforms were implemented in rural areas. From 1952 to 1957 the government carried out a series of collectivization campaigns and finally established People's Communes in 1958, which abolished private ownership of the means of production in rural regions. Peasants lost their land ownership and became wage earners in their production teams under the People's Commune.[40]

In cities, the government nationalized private industry and commerce between 1956 and 1957. Many urban residents became state employees. The land reforms, the collectivization campaigns, and the nationalization campaigns eliminated the propertied classes and destroyed the old class structure in China. There was virtually no private ownership of the means of production in Mainland China, except in Tibet, between 1957 and 1978.[41]

Nevertheless, "class" designations and political role labels persisted and were grouped together after 1957. The government threw landlords, rich peasants, counterrevolutionaries, "bad elements" and rightists together to create a listing of the "five bad elements".[42] The official practice of grouping together the political labels and the "class" designations lasted till 1979 and generated three caste-like political status groups:

1. the "good class" (workers, poor and lower middle peasants, revolutionary armymen, cadres, etc.);
2. the "middle class" (intellectuals, professionals, clerks, peddlers, middle peasants, etc.);
3. the "bad class" (landlors, rich peasants, capitalists, "bad elements", rightists, etc.).

The Social Significance of the "Class" Labeling

As time passed by, the government considered family "class" designations and political labels inheritable along the male line. One famous slogan of the Cultural Revolution was that "if the father is a hero, so is his son; if the father is a reactionary, his son is a good-for-nothing".[43] Family political status became an important factor of social stratification in the Mao era, influencing a person's life chances and determining his or her rights to participate in the political process.[44] The government reserved certain occupations, e.g., the military service, for people of the "good class".

In addition, family political status came to be a factor in mate choices. "Good class" women did not want to marry "bad class" males. Their social standing would be downgraded it they did.[45] Family political status was also related to Red Guard factionalism. Children of cadre families were more likely to support the existing political system than children of the "bad class" and "middle class". Children of the "good class" denied Red Guard membership to students with the "bad class" origin, who in turn challenged the official policy of "class" designations.[46] Political labels and "class" designations became a caste-like ordering of honor and shame that dominated both the popular and official consciousness until 1979.[47]

Notes

1. Richard Kraus, *Class Conflict in Chinese Socialism* (New York: Columbia University Press, 1981).

2. Etienne Balasz, *Chinese Civilization and Bureaucracy* (New Haven: Yale University Press, 1974); Chung-li Chang, *The Chinese Gentry* (Seattle: University of Washington Press, 1955); Hsiao-tung Fei, *China's Gentry* (Chicago: The University of Chicago Press, 1980); Ping-Ti Ho, *The Ladder of Success in Imperial China* (New York: Columbia University Press, 1962).

3. Chang 1955 (footnote 2), Pp. 116-119; 139; Gilbert Razman, *Urban Network in Ch'ing China and Tokugawa Japan* (Princeton: Princeton University Press, 1973), Pp. 6 & 88.

4. Chang 1955 (footnote 2); Fei 1980 (footnote 2); Ho 1962 (footnote 2).

5. Li Zhu, "*Shixi Woguo Naotishouru Bizhong de Shiheng.*" (An Analysis of Causes for Unfair Distribution of Income between Mental and Manual Workers in Our Country)." *Lanzhou Xuekan* (1991) no. 2: Pp. 65-70; Zhen Yefu, "*Woguo Naoti Shouru Chabie De Lishi Bianqian Jiqi Fanxing.*" (Reflections on the Historical Development of the Unfair Distribution of Income between Mental and Manual Workers in Our Country)." *Shijie Jingji Daobao* (May 1985) no. 9: p. 15.

6. Chang 1955 (footnote 2); Fei 1980 (footnote 2); Ho 1962 (footnote 2).

7. Ch'u T'ung-tsu, "Chinese Class Structure and Its Ideology." Pp. 235-250 in John K. Fairbank (ed.) *Chinese Thought and Institutions* (Chicago: University of Chicago Press, 1957); Mark Elvin, *The Pattern of the Chinese Past* (Stanford: Stanford University Press, 1973), p. 248; Ho 1962 (footnote 2), Pp. 18-19, 55-56; Philip A. Kuhn, "Chinese Views of Social Classification." Pp. 16-28 in James L. Watson (ed.) *Class and Social Stratification in Post-Revolution China* (Cambridge: Cambridge University Press, 1984).

8. Ch'u 1957 (footnote 7); Elvin 1973 (footnote 7); Ho 1962 (footnote 2); Kuhn 1984 (footnote 7).

9. Ch'u 1957 (footnote 7); Elvin 1973 (footnote 7); Ho 1962 (footnote 2); Kuhn 1984 (footnote 7).

10. Yen-p'ing Hao, *The Commercial Revolution in Nineteenth-Century China* (Berkeley: University of California Press, 1986); Ernest R. May and John K. Fairbank (eds.), *America's China Trade in Historical Perspective* (The Council on East Asian Studies, Harvard University, 1986); John K. Fairbank, *Trade and Diplomacy on the China Coast* (Cambridge: Harvard University Press, 1969).

11. Marie-Claire Bergere, *The Golden Age of the Chinese Bourgeoisie, 1911-1937* (Cambridge: Cambridge University Press, 1989); Olga Lang, *Chinese Family and Society* (New Haven: Yale University Press, 1946); Thomas G. Rawski, *Economic Growth in Prewar China* (Berkeley: University of California Press, 1989).

12. Bergere 1989 (footnote 11); Lang 1946 (footnote 11).

13. Bergere 1989 (footnote 11); Lang 1946 (footnote 11).

14. Bergere 1989 (footnote 11); Rawski 1989 (footnote 11).

15. Rawski 1989 (footnote 11).

16. Rawski 1989 (footnote 11).

17. Audrey Donnithorne, *China's Economic System* (London: George Allen and Unwin Ltd., 1967), Chapter 1. An article in *People's Daily* (oversees edition, January 27,

1992, p. 8) claimed that before 1937, 55 percent of the rural population were landless peasants. Landlords and rich peasants accounted for less than 15 percent of the rural population but owned 81 percent of the land under cultivation.

18. Mao Zedong, "An Analysis of the Classes in Chinese Society." Pp. 3-11 in Zhonggong Zhongyang Mao Zedong Xuanji Chuban Weiyuanhui (ed.) *Mao Zedong Xuanji* (Selected Works of Mao Zedong) (Beijing: People's Press, 1969).

19. Mao 1969 (footnote 18).

20. Lang 1946 (footnote 11).

21. Lang did not explain whether the dollar signs referred to Chinese currency.

22. Lang 1946 (footnote 11).

23. Lang 1946 (footnote 11).

24. Lang 1946 (footnote 11).

25. Lang 1946 (footnote 11).

26. Li 1991 (footnote 5); Zhen 1985 (footnote 5). The dollar signs here refer to Chinese currency.

27. Li 1991 (footnote 5); Zhen 1985 (footnote 5).

28. Yichu Wang, "Western Impact and Social Mobility in China." *American Sociological Review* (1960) 25: Pp. 843-855.

29. Suzanne Pepper, *Civil War in China: The Political Struggle, 1945-49* (Berkeley: University of California Press, 1978).

30. Pepper 1978 (footnote 29).

31. Chen Zhili, *Zhongguo Gongchandang Jiandangshi* (A History of the Chinese Communist Party) (Shanghai: Shanghai Renming Chubanshe, 1991); James Pinckney Harrison, *The Long March to Power: A History of the Chinese Communist Party, 1921-1972* (New York: Praeger, 1972); Hong Yung Lee, *From Revolutionary Cadres to Party Technocrats in Socialist China* (Berkeley: University of California Press, 1991).

32. William Hinton, *Fanshen* (New York: Vintage Books, 1966); Vivienne Shue, *Peasant China in Transition* (Berkeley: University of California Press, 1980); Helen Siu, *Agents and Victims in South China* (New Haven: Yale University Press, 1989); John Wong, *Land Reform in the People's Republic of China* (New York: Praeger, 1973); Xue Muqiao, *China's Socialist Economy* (Beijing: Foreign Languages Press, 1981).

33. Library Section, The Institute of Philosophy, China Social Sciences Academy, *Sanshinian Jieji he Jiejidouzheng Lunwen Xuanji* (Selected Works on Class and Class Struggle for the Past 30 Years) (Beijing: China Social Sciences Academy, 1980), p. 694.

34. Hinton 1966 (footnote 32); Siu 1989 (footnote 32); Wong 1973 (footnote 32); Xu 1981 (footnote 32).

35. Library Section 1980 (footnote 33), p. 694; Su Ji and Jia Lusheng, *Bai Mao Hei Mao, Zhongguo Gaige Xianzhuang Toushi* (White Cats and Black Cats, The Current Situations of China's Economic Reform) (Changsha: Hunan Renming Chubanshe, 1992), Pp. 42-43.

36. Library Section 1980 (footnote 33), p. 692; Su and Jia 1992 (footnote 35).

37. Library Section 1980 (footnote 33), p. 692; Su and Jia 1992 (footnote 35).

38. Kraus 1981(footnote 1); Library Section 1980 (footnote 33), p. 694. There were also "good" political labels such as revolutionary army men, revolutionary martyrs, and revolutionary cadres.

39. For information on the 1957 Anti-Rightists Campaign, see Roderick MacFarquhar, *Origins of the Cultural Revolution Vol. I* (New York: Columbia University Press, 1974); Mu Fu-sheng, *The Wilting of the Hundred Flowers: the Chinese Intelligentsia under Mao* (New York: Praeger, 1963).

40. See Parris H. Chang, *Power and Policy in China* (University Park: The Pennsylvania State University Press, 1975); Philip C. C. Huang, *The Peasant Family and Rural Development in the Yangzi Delta, 1350-1988* (Stanford: Stanford University Press, 1990); Sulamith Potter and Jack M. Potter, *China's Peasants* (Cambridge and New York: Cambridge University Press, 1990); Shue 1980 (footnote 32); Frederick C. Teiwes and Warren Sun (eds.) *The Politics of Agricultural Cooperativization in China* (Armonk: M. E. Sharpe, 1993); Yunxiang Yan, *The Flow of Gifts* (Stanford: Stanford University Press, 1996), p. 29.

41. Xue 1981 (footnote 32).

42. Jean-Francois Billeter, "The System of 'Class Status'." Pp. 127-169 in Stuart R. Scharm (ed.) *The Scope of State Power in China* (London: School of Oriental and African Studies, University of London, 1985); Kraus 1981(footnote 1); Hong Yung Lee, *The Politics of the Cultural Revolution* (Berkeley: University of California Press, 1978); Stanley Rosen, *Red Guard Factionalism and the Cultural Revolution in Guangzhou* (Boulder: Westview Press, 1982); Jonathan Unger, "The Class System in Rural China." Pp. 121-141 in Watson 1984 (footnote 7); Gordon White, *The Politics of Class and Class Origins* (Contemporary China Centre, The Australian National University, 1974).

43. See Billeter 1985 (footnote 42), p. 134.

44. Lee 1978 (footnote 42); Rosen 1982 (footnote 42); White 1974 (footnote 42); Mayfair Mei-hui Yang, *Gifts, Favors, and Banquets* (Ithaca: Cornell University Press, 1994), p. 186.

45. Elizabeth Croll, *The Politics of Marriage in Contemporary China* (Cambridge: Cambridge University Press, 1981).

46. Lee 1978 (footnote 42); Rosen 1982 (footnote 42); White 1974 (footnote 42).

47. Kraus 1981 (footnote 1).

3

JOB RANKING AND SOCIAL CLASSES

I have discussed in Chapter 2 how the socialist transformation campaign of 1949-1957 eliminated private ownership of the means of production. A family political status system was set up and came to be an important dimension of stratification in Mao's China. However, stratification by family political status was unable to fully reflect the rich complexity of inequalities in the Mao era. Since 1956, the state sector dominated the Chinese economy. The government established a job ranking system to remunerate state employees. Occupational ranking, as Richard Kraus points out, became a better index to economic position than the pre-1949 class status.[1] I show in this chapter that occupational ranking also determined the distribution of status and prestige among state employees. The job ranking system became the basis of class formation in the Mao era.

The Growth of Urban Work Force in China

The 1949 Communist Takeover marked the beginning of a government sponsored industrialization program and a concomitant rapid expansion of the urban work force during the 1950s and the 1960s. In 1952 there were only 17.3 million laborers in the primary sector, 1.5 million in the secondary sector and 1.9 million in the tertiary sector. By 1965 the corresponding figures were 24 million, 2.6 million, and 2.9 million respectively.[2] In 1952, the state sector employed 15.8 million workers only. By 1965, they commanded a 37.38 million strong labor force (Table 3.1). The total number of technicians, engineers and managers in the state sector was nearly doubled from 893,600 in 1952 to 1.6 million in 1965.[3]

Concurrently, China's urban population grew from less than 58 million in 1949 to more than 133 million in 1965. In other words, the proportion represented by urban residents increased from 10.6 percent in 1949 to 17.9 percent of the total population in 1966 (Table 3.2).

The number of administrative bureaucrats and professionals increased significantly with the rapid expansion of the urban population and the industrial labor force. Party cadres and government officials numbered 5.3 million in 1952; 8 million in 1958; and 11.6 million in 1965.[4] Only half a million doctors and other medical personnel practised medicine in China on the eve of the 1949 Communist Takeover. By 1965 the medical profession claimed a membership of 1.5 million.[5] It was estimated that 16,000 professors taught at universities before 1949. When the Cultural Revolution took place in 1966 the higher education sector hired more than 138,000 teaching staff.[6] The total number of scientists and technicians in research institutes increased from 425,000 in 1952 to 1.9 million in 1960.[7] Based on these figures, a very conservative estimate of professionals and government officials would point to a figure of over 15 million in 1966.

TABLE 3.1 Work Force in China: 1952-1966 (in 10,000s)

Year	State Unit	Urban Collective	Total
1952	1,580	23	1,603
1953	1,826	30	1,856
1954	1,881	121	2,002
1955	1,908	254	2,162
1956	2,423	554	2,977
1957	2,451	650	3,101
1958	4,532	662	5,194
1959	4,561	714	5,275
1960	5,044	925	5,969
1961	4,171	1,000	5,171
1962	3,309	1,012	4,321
1963	3,293	1,079	4,372
1964	3,465	1,136	4,601
1965	3,738	1,227	4,965
1966	3,934	1,264	5,198

Source: State Statistical Bureau, People's Republic of China, *Zhongguo Tongji Nianjian 1981*. (China Statistical Yearbook 1981) (Hong Kong: Jingji Daobaoshe, 1982), p. 107.

Economic Development and Social Inequality

According to Marxist theory, socialist revolution aims not only at social upheaval and inversion, but also at economic development. An egalitarian communist society is attainable only when there is abundant material wealth. Marx predicts that the working class victory over capitalism will occur in advanced European capitalist countries as industrialization there has created the necessary material condition for the occurrence of socialist revolution.

Nevertheless, most socialist victories have taken place in traditional peasant societies (e.g., China, Vietnam and North Korea) characterized by poverty, scarcity of resources, backwardness and war destruction. Once political control is firmly assured, economic development becomes the highest priority of every communist government in the world. Economic development, however, produces social inequality and class differentiation in socialist society.[8]

Needless to say, communist regimes often rely on coercion to mobilize the masses. Coercion alone however is insufficient to guarantee adequate servicing of a rapidly industrializing economy. Nor can it motivate people to train for much needed skills. The communist regimes tend to reward those who contribute to economic development and punish those who fail to compete. Demands of economic growth give rise to a reward structure in socialist societies similar to that of capitalist societies. Patterns of social stratification in income, prestige and power in socialist societies do not deviate very much from those in Western societies.[9]

TABLE 3.2 Urban Population in China: 1949-1966

Year	Population (Millions)	Percent of Total Population
1949	57.6	10.6
1950	61.7	11.2
1951	66.3	11.8
1952	71.6	12.5
1953	78.2	13.3
1954	82.5	13.7
1955	82.9	13.5
1956	91.9	14.6
1957	99.5	15.4
1958	107.2	16.2
1959	123.7	18.4
1960	130.7	19.7
1961	127.1	19.3
1962	116.6	17.3
1963	116.5	16.8
1964	129.5	18.4
1965	130.1	18.0
1966	133.1	17.9

Source: State Statistical Bureau, *Zhongguo Tongji Nianjian 1983* (China Statistical Yearbook 1983) (Hong Kong: Jingji Daobaoshe, 1983), Pp. 103-104.

In fact, Mao Zedong, Chairman of the CCP, had an excellent understanding of the need for social stratification. As early as 1929 he argued against "absolute egalitarianism" in the Red Army, asserting that because officers held important positions and made a great contribution to the survival and expansion of the Red Army, they deserved a higher amount of remuneration than foot soldiers in the ranks.[10]

Other top CCP leaders held similar views. Ever since the establishment of the People's Republic of China, the CCP has consistently carried on the principle of distribution according to labor, a principle of inequality in reality. State employees (workers, intellectuals, professionals, cadres, etc.) were given different amounts of material rewards since their contribution to socialism was perceived by the CCP to be different.[11]

The Job Ranking System

Inequality in income, occupational prestige and status in Mao's China was primarily based on a job ranking system established between 1949 and 1957. When the CCP rose to power in 1949, there had been two remuneration systems in urban China.

First, workers, professionals and intellectuals received wages or salaries from their current employers, whether public or private. Second, government employees who had joined the revolution before October 1, 1949 were compensated through a de facto system of payment in kind that had already existed prior to 1949; those who started to work for the communist government after October 1, 1949 could choose to join the payment in kind system or receive a monthly cash payment. Most newly-recruited state employees chose the payment in king system since it was widely perceived as a symbol of communism.[12]

The system of payment in kind was formally promulgated in January 1950. It was modified in 1952 and 1954. There were three basic components in this remuneration system: free meals, clothing and a small amount of spare money.[13]

From July 1955 onward, the central government gradually eliminated the system of payment in kind and placed all state employees under a wage system. This plan was finalized on April 1, 1956 with the promulgation of a new wage system by the central government.[14]

The 1956 wage system covered virtually every state employee, up to President of the People's Republic of China and down to directors of the People's Communes in the countryside. Each was given some sort of job ranking, regardless of whether he or she worked in a government agency, a department store, an urban state factory, a state plant located in the countryside or a state farming unit.[15]

The 1956 wage system was extremely complex. Employees of different trades were placed under different wage grade systems. Blue-collar workers were awarded in a workers' system, government officials and functionaries in a cadres' system, educators in an educators' system and school administrators in an education administrators' system.[16]

Each wage system contained a number of grades. For example, cadres were classified into thirty grades (Table 3.3). The law enforcement system contained thirteen grades and the workers' system eight grades. College professors were stratified into thirteen grades, middle school teachers into ten grades, and primary school teachers into eleven grades. Engineers were differentiated by an eight-point salary scale and technicians by a five-point scale.[17]

TABLE 3. 3 Grades, Positions, and Wages under the 1956 Wage System (Cadres in Beijing)

Grade	Position	Monthly Wage
1-2	Chairman and vice chairmen of the Central Government, chairman and vice chairmen of the People's Congress, prime minister, deputy prime ministers, president of the Supreme People's Court, and procurator-general of the Supreme People's Procuratorate	644-581
3-8	Ministers, vice ministers, vice presidents of the Supreme People's Court, deputy procurators-general of the Supreme People's Procuratorate, heads and deputy heads of divisions, provincial governors and deputy provincial governors and their equivalents	517.5-287.5
9	Chiefs and deputy chiefs of divisions, provincial governors and deputy provincial governors, heads and deputy heads of divisions, judges and their equivalents	253
10-14	Heads and deputy heads of prefectures, heads and deputy heads of departments under the division, judges, county magistrates and deputy magistrates, city mayors and deputy mayors, judges and their equivalents	218.5-138
15-18	County magistrates and deputy magistrates, city mayors and deputy city mayors, heads and deputy heads of bureaus and their equivalents	124-87.5
19-21	Bureau officers, heads and deputies of townships, court clerks and their equivalents	78-62
22-27	Bureau clerks, heads and deputies of townships and their equivalents	56-30
28-30	Service personnel	27.5-23

Source: State Personnel Bureau, *Renshi Gongzuo Wenjian Xuanbian, Vol. II* (A Selection of Documents on Personnel Management in China, Vol. II) (Beijing: Laodong Renshi Chubanshe, 1986), Pp. 6-7.

TABLE 3.4 Grades and Monthly Wages by Districts: 1956–1985

Grade	District										
	1	2	3	4	5	6	7	8	9	10	11
1	560	577	593.5	610.5	627	644	661	677.5	694.5	711	729
2	505	520	535.5	550.5	565.5	581	596	611	626	641.5	656.5
3	450	463.5	477	490.5	504	517.5	531	544.5	558	571.5	585
4	400	412	424	436	448	460	472	484	496	508	520
5	360	371	381.5	392.5	403	414	425	435	446.5	457	468
6	320	329.5	339	349	358.5	368	377.5	387	397	406.5	416
7	280	288.5	297	305	313.5	322	330.5	339	347	355.5	364
8	250	257.5	265	272.5	280	287.5	295	302.5	310	317.5	325
10	190	195.5	201.5	207	213	218	224	230	235.5	241.5	247
11	170	175	180	185.5	190.5	195.5	200.5	205.5	211	216	221
12	150	154.5	159	163.5	168	172.5	177	181.5	186	190.5	195
13	135	139	143	147	151	155.5	159.5	163.5	167.5	171.5	175.5
15	108	111	114.5	117.5	121	124	127.5	130.5	134	137	140.5
16	96	99	102	104.5	107.5	110.5	113.5	116	119	122	125
17	86	88.5	91	93.5	96.5	99	101.5	104	106.5	109	112
18	76	78.5	80.5	83	85	87.5	89.5	92	94	96.5	99
20	61	63	64.5	66.5	68.5	70	72	74	75.5	77.5	79.5
22	48.5	50	51.5	53	54.5	56	57	58.5	60	61.5	63
30	20	20.5	21	22	22.5	23	23.5	24	25	25.5	26

Source: State Personnel Bureau, *Renshi Gongzuo Wenjian Xuanbian, Vol. II* (A Selection of Documents on Personnel Management in China, Vol. II) (Beijing: Laodong Renshi Chubanshe, 1986), p. 6.

A twenty grades award scheme applied to employees in the news media industry and a twenty-one grades system to those in the public health system. Professional athletes might attain fourteen ranks. The entertainment industry boasted a twenty-four grades wage system.[18]

Different criteria were used in deciding each state employee's wage grade. An educator's grade was determined on the basis of his or her pre-1949 salary and professional title; a worker's grade, of his or her wage history and seniority in the workforce; a cadre's grade, of the combination of his or her position in the government or the CCP, his or her seniority in party membership and his or her contribution to the Chinese Communist Revolution.[19]

Labor market mobility between different industries or occupations was not a big problem for the 1956 wage system. The People's Republic of China in the Mao era was a China Inc. as the CCP ran both the state economy and the government. Job transfers among the government system, enterprises and other state agencies resembled reassignments inside a big corporation.

For example, the director of the industrial bureau in a city might be sent to head a bureau level state enterprise. A factory gatekeeper might be assigned to work in the factory's canteen. If a cadre or a worker were transferred to a different wage grade system, he or she would be given a comparable grade in the new system.

Finally, the government divided China into eleven districts according to costs of living (Table 3.4).[20] For example, both Xiamen City in Fujian Province and Shanghai City belonged to District Eight, Beijing City belonged to District Six, Lasha City in Tibet belonged to District Eleven. The wage system was then placed within the eleven-district framework so that each wage grade had eleven scales.

Take a cadre of grade fifteen for an example: his or her monthly salary in District One was $124;[21] in District Eight, $130.5; in District Eleven, $140.5. If transferred from Shanghai (District Eight) to Beijing (District Six), he or she would suffer on paper a $6.5 loss per month.[22] But his or her actual living standard might not be affected by the loss since the cost of living in Beijing was lower than that in Shanghai.

The cluster of wage-grades remained unchanged throughout the Mao era in its basic structure,[23] stratifying state employees into several distinct groups. Each was given a place in the social hierarchy with specific rights to income, status, prestige and other benefits; each, in other words, was entitled to a distinctive living standard.

Peasants were excluded from the wage grade system, although they stood for over 80 percent of the total population in the Mao era. After the 1957 collectivization campaign, peasants were organized into production teams, which were incorporated into production brigades under the People's Commune. The production team replaced the family as the basic accounting unit in rural China. Peasants farmed for their production teams and earned work points. At the end of each year they received grains, other products and money from their production teams on the basis of the number of work points they had accumulated throughout the year. Some peasants were engaged in sideline production on their small private lots of land to supplement their income.[24]

TABLE 3.5 Examples of Wage Districts: 1956-1985

Province	District					
	1	3	5	7	9	11
Shanxi			Taiyuan			
Neimenggu			Jining	Xilinhaote		Bayinzuoer
Liaoning			Jinzhou	Changhai		
Heilongjiang			Fuyuan		Heihe	
Jilin			Siping		Changbai	
Shaaxi	Hanyin	Ankang		Weinan		
Hebei			Tangshan			
Qinghai						Qinghai
Shandong			Changdao			
Jiangsu		Haibei	Songjiiang			
Zhejiang				Zhoushan		
Fujian			Jianyang	Fuzhou		
Henan		Kaifeng				
Hunan		Changsha				
Jiangxi		Nanchang				
Guangdong			Shaoguan	Shantao		Hainan
Guangxi			Nanning			
Sichuan	Neijiang	Yaan	Muli		Meigu	Ganzi
Guizhou	Xingyi	Guiyang				
Yunnan	Shaotong	Xiaguan				

Source: State Personnel Bureau, *Renshi Gongzuo Wenjian Xuanbian, Vol. II* (A Selection of Documents on Personnel Management in China, Vol. II) (Beijing: Laodong Renshi Chubanshe, 1986), Pp. 23-36.

Income differences between production teams and geographical regions existed. Rich peasants in the most affluent regions were still poor compared to urban workers. Unlike peasants, urban state workers enjoyed high wages, job security, housing subsidies, medical care, pensions and many other fringe benefits.[25]

Throughout the Mao era peasants were systematically deprived of their economic and political rights. During most of the periods the CCP's development policies sought to bring about high levels of rural savings and limited consumption so as to facilitate industrialization and urbanization. Not surprisingly, rural incomes were substantially lower than urban incomes. The ratio of peasant incomes to worker incomes was 1 : 3.2 in 1957 and 1: 2.1 in 1965.[26] Income difference between urban workers and rural peasants was enlarged again during the Cultural Revolution. By the 1970s the ratio of rural incomes to urban incomes was 1 : 3.[27] Peasants became part of the lower class in Mao's China.

Income Differentiation

The job ranking system created highly structured income inequality in the state sector. Under the 1956 wage system, state employees of different grades were subject to different scales of remuneration.[28]

For the sake of convenience and consistency, wage scales in District One (Table 3.4) are used in the following illustration. In that wage district, the monthly salary for a grade one cadre was $560; for a grade ten cadre, $190; for a grade fifteen cadre, $108; for a grade twenty cadre, $61; and for a grade thirty cadre, $20.[29]

In the same district, the monthly pay for a grade one engineer was $290; for a grade six engineer, $137; for a grade twelve engineer, $54; and for a grade eighteen engineer, $24. In the university professors' wage system, a grade one professor earned $300 per month; a grade four professor, $180; and a grade twelve professor, $54.[30]

Thus, there were substantial income differences between different grades within each wage system. A grade one cadre made twenty-eight times more than a cadre of grade thirty. The monthly salary for a grade one professor was 5.6 times of that of a teaching assistant of grade twelve.[31] One's wage grade, rather than his or her occupation or actual work, determined his or her income. While high ranking cadres earned the highest salaries, low ranking cadres were, together with manual workers and peasants, placed at the bottom of the income hierarchy.

The income of senior intellectuals and professionals was comparable to that of high cadres. The monthly salary range for a minister or a deputy minister was from $400 to $250; for a provincial governor or a deputy provincial governor, from $360 to $220; and for a county magistrate or a deputy county magistrate, from $135 to $76.[32]

In comparison, full professors earned between $300 and $130 per month; associate professors, between $210 and $130; and lecturers, between $130 and $78.[33] Intellectuals and professionals did rather well financially as compared with workers and low ranking cadres.[34]

Additionally, the government took good care of intellectuals and professionals. For example, in order to make sure all lecturers and professors at Xiamen University survived a 1962 famine, the Fujian provincial government issued them coupons for an extra amount of food on top of their rations.[35]

TABLE 3.6 Grades and Wages of Engineers and Technicians by Districts: 1956-1985

Grade	District										
	1	2	3	4	5	6	7	8	9	10	11
1	290	298.5	307.5	316	325	333.5	342	351	359.5	368.5	377
2	250	257.5	265	272.5	280	287.5	295	302.5	310	317.5	325
3	215	221.5	228	234.5	241	247.5	253.5	260	266.5	273	279.5
4	185	190.5	196	201.5	207	213	218.5	224	229.5	235	240.5
5	159	164	168.5	173.5	178	183	187.5	192.5	197	202	206.5
6	137	141	145	149.5	153.5	157.5	161.5	166	170	174	178
7	118	121.5	125	128.5	132	135.5	139	143	146.5	150	153.5
8	102	105	108	111	114	117.5	120.5	123.5	126.5	129.5	132.5
9	89	91.5	94.5	97	99.5	102.5	105	107.5	110.5	113	115.5
10	77	79.5	81.5	84	86	88.5	91	93	95.5	98	100
11	65	67	69	71	73	75	76.5	78.5	80.5	82.5	84.5
12	54	55.5	57	59	60.5	62	63.5	65.5	67	68.5	70
13	48	49.5	51	52.5	54	55	56.5	58	59.5	61	62.5

Note: Senior Engineers (grade 1 to grade 4); engineers (grade 3 to grade 9); technicians (grade 9 to grade 13). Source: State Personnel Bureau, *Renshi Gongzuo Wenjian Xuanbian, Vol. II* (A Selection of Documents on Personnel Management in China, Vol. II) (Beijing: Laodong Renshi Chubanshe, 1986), p. 15.

Workers did not receive similar treatments. Most of them were hired at or below grade four and made $30-$40 per month,[36] which was substantially lower than the starting salary of university graduates (approximately $50 per month).

Existing studies of income inequality in Mao's China show that the wage grade system provides a base line for understanding income inequality before the Cultural Revolution. Martin King Whyte and William L. Parish report that the average monthly income for state employees was $46; for metropolitan neighborhood factory employees, $39; for township collective workshop employees, $37; and for self-employed workers, $35.[37]

William L. Parish finds out that senior professionals were second in income only to high-ranking CCP and government cadres. Factory and store managers earned much less. Personal income was smaller down through accountants, teachers, nurses, office clerks, postmen, cashiers, sales clerks and other low professionals. Next in line were drivers, transport workers and other skilled workers, all financially better off than barbers, cooks, waiters, ordinary and semi-skilled blue-collar workers. On the bottom rungs of the income ladder were street cleaners, apprentices, housemaids and other unskilled and casual laborers.[38]

Martin King Whyte agrees with Parish's assessment of the income structure in the Mao era, pointing out that high-ranking professionals and senior officials were at the top of the wage hierarchy under Mao, state workers were at the bottom.[39]

Thus, the remuneration scheme in Mao's China was similar to the wage structure in the West, with manual workers, low professionals and low officials falling in the low income category; middle-ranking professionals and officials in the middle income category; and high professionals and high officials in the high income category.

Official Status

Mao's China was a status-conscious society. Social Status was based on the 1956 job ranking system. Before it came to power in 1949, the CCP had already set up a status system within itself and the PLA. A person's status in the CCP or the PLA was determined by his or her position and seniority in party membership. This status system was reflected in a "mess" system, which was officially proclaimed in January 1950.[40]

Under this system, cadres holding positions up to Chairman of the CCP and President of the People's Republic of China and down to county magistrates and their equivalents were entitled to eat a "special mess". Cadres holding positions up to deputy county magistrates, reporters, doctors, accountants, actors, and their equivalents and those who had worked in their professions for eight years consecutively ate a "good mess." All low-placed personnel such as drivers ate an "ordinary mess".

In 1952, the government's subsidy for the "special mess" was 645.3 wage points per person; for the "good mess", 112.3 wage points per person; and for "ordinary mess", 37 wage points per person.[41] Needless to say, the "special mess" prepared the best food; the "good mess", good food; and the "ordinary mess", ordinary food.

The "mess" system was abolished in 1955. However, its principle of stratification was inherited in the 1956 job ranking wage system and transformed into an official status system. Cadres of grade one to grade thirteen were officially classified as high ranking cadres (*Gaoji Ganbu*); those of grade fourteen down to grade seventeen, middle ranking cadres (*Zhongceng Ganbu*); and those of grade eighteen and below, low ranking cadres *(Xiaceng Ganbu or jiceng Ganbu)*. PLA officers of comparable grades were also classified into the three categories.[42]

Intellectuals and professionals were similarly classified into three categories. "High ranking intellectuals" included professors of grade one to grade four and their equivalents in other professions (e.g., senior doctors, chief engineers, leading writers); "middle ranking intellectuals" included professors of grade five to grade nine (e.g., junior full professors, associate professors and lecturers) and their equivalents in other professions (e.g., doctors, engineers, editors, reporters). "Low ranking intellectuals" (e.g., primary school teachers) and other low professionals (e.g., assistant engineers and technicians) were placed at the bottom of the status hierarchy.

Government regulations defined a state employee's privileges on the basis of his or her official status. For example, Marshal Lin Biao, vice chairman of the CCP and the officially designated successor to Chairman Mao Zedong, developed serious disagreements with Mao over a number of issues after 1969. Lin came to realize that his position in the CCP was insecure and decided to assassinate Chairman Mao in 1971. After his plot was aborted, the CCP leadership informed high ranking cadres first, middle ranking cadres second, and low ranking cadres and ordinary citizens lastly.

As another example, high ranking cadres had access to *International Reference* (*Dacankao*), which was an internal publication of classified documents and international affairs. They were well informed of international politics and domestic situations.[43]

Middle ranking cadres read *Internal Reference* (*Cankaoxiaoxi*), which was also an internal publication but contained less classified information. Low ranking cadres could only subscribe *People's Daily,* which was also available to ordinary citizens. Most junior cadres and ordinary citizens did not know the existence of *International Reference* and *Internal Reference*.[44]

Leading cadres had better housing than middle ranking cadres, whose housing condition in turn was better than that of junior cadres and ordinary citizens. Most high ranking cadres had access to cars, security guards, and service personnel. They received extra ration coupons for food and clothing from the government during the 1960s and the 1970s.

High ranking cadres were allowed to travel by air or on "soft-bed" passenger carriages (*Ruanwoche*), which had seats similar to sofa beds. Those holding middle ranking positions in the CCP or the government travelled on "hard-bed" passenger carriages (*Yingwoche*), which had small wooden beds. Junior cadres had to sit in wooden benches in "ordinary" passenger carriages with ordinary citizens and had no bed to sleep on.[45]

This system of privilege distribution applied to other professions and the PLA. For example, PLA division commanders and their equivalents could read *International Reference* and travel by air or on "soft-bed" passenger carriages. PLA regiment commanders and their equivalents could read *Internal Reference* and travel on "hard-bed" passenger carriages. Professors of grade four and up to grade one enjoyed similar traveling privileges to those of high ranking cadres. Those of grade five to grade nine had same traveling privileges as middle ranking cadres did.

Occupational Prestige

Virtually all the comparative studies of transnational occupational prestige show that all societies construct roughly similar occupational prestige hierarchies. It does not make a great difference whether these societies are industrial or "traditional". Socialist societies do deviate somewhat from other societies in their patterns of prestige allocation, but not so radically as to constitute a different world.[46]

In Mao's China, according to Susan Shirk, at the top of the Chinese status ranking were non-manual professionals such as doctors, research scientists, university professors, engineers, factory technicians, and government and party officials. They were followed by skilled urban factory workers, who in turn were ranked higher than unskilled workers. Employees working in heavy industry enjoyed more prestige than those in light industry, who in turn scored higher than workers in the service industry. On the bottom rungs of the status ladder were rural peasants.[47]

There was differentiation in prestige within low ranking professionals as well. Technicians, junior engineers, and their equivalents with university education were ranked higher on the prestige scale than low teaching personnel in primary, junior-middle, and "people-run" schools. Workers in state firms were also ranked higher than these low teaching personnel, who earned less money than the junior members of other professions.[48] Overall, the status structure in Mao's China was similar to that in the West.

Results of the surveys on occupational prestige conducted in post-Mao China (1979 and 1983) also reveal a striking similarity between the job prestige hierarchy in China and that in the West. Post-Mao reforms had not generated significant social changes during the period of 1979-1983. The results of these surveys may be used as a rough index of the prestige scale predating the Cultural Revolution.

In these surveys, the highest prestige ratings generally apply to high-level professional jobs (university professors, doctors, and the like) that are also rated high in Western industrial societies. The low-rated occupations such as construction workers and waiters are in the unskilled manual categories, which are also rated lower in the West.[49]

These surveys also show the difference in prestige within each occupational group. For example, Nan Lin and Wen Xie report that in their occupational prestige scale, high ranking cadres scored 72.9 points; middle ranking cadres, 67.4 points; and low ranking cadres, 63.2 points. Similarly, university professors have a higher job prestige score (83.8 points) than secondary school teachers (79.4 pints), who in turn have a higher prestige score than primary school teachers (60.1 points).[50]

Since the collectivization campaign of 1956-1957, peasants stayed at the bottom of the socioeconomic hierarchy in China and enjoyed little respect. A survey of primary school students in Wuxi City, Jiangsu Province, conducted in November 1979, showed that only four out of 839 respondents chose "peasant/farmer" when asked what work they would like to do when they grew up. In another survey of 1,122 urban and rural middle school students in Liaoning Province in 1980, only two listed "peasant" as their "ideal future occupation".[51]

The occupational prestige structure ran roughly parallel to the income hierarchy. Leading cadres and professionals earned the highest wages and were ranked the highest in the job prestige hierarchy. Middle ranking professionals and cadres were in the middle of the wage structure and the prestige scale. Junior cadres and professionals, workers, poor and lower middle peasants—the so-called "masters of the state"—were poor and had low prestige. This prestige pattern is not very different from that in Western societies and other Asian societies.[52]

Choices of Mates

Inequality in income, prestige, and status also reflected in mate choices in Mao's China. Elizabeth Croll reports that high ranking government officials and professionals made up the positive poles of the socioeconomic status gradient in the marriage market. Next were junior cadres, low professionals, and skilled workers. Unskilled workers were better off than peasants, who were on the negative pole of the socioeconomic status and were considered the least desirable mate perspectives.[53]

Some unskilled male workers, especially those who came from rural areas, had a hard time finding suitable mates in urban areas. They thus married female peasants in their home villages. Few female urban residents would marry male peasants.

Classes in Mao's China

Karl Marx defines classes in terms of positions in production (i.e., access to property, money and wealth). Max Weber identifies two additional social hierarchies: (1) status groups, which refer to groups with different lifestyles, values, beliefs, and manners of living, and are distinguished by different levels of honor or social prestige; (2) party, which is a political organization formed by people of common political interests and same objectives of achieving specific goals.[54] Weber's insistence on separating the economic from the social and political dimensions underlines his belief that the three hierarchies do not necessarily overlap. However, the possibility of economic, political, and social convergence is always there.

For example, in the US and some Asian societies, middle class people tend to have higher income and prestige than lower class people. This is because middle class people tend to be better educated than lower class people. Educational achievement is an important factor for upward mobility in the market place. Education, income, and prestige are correlated with one another and form the basis upon which classes are delineated.

In their research on social stratification, many scholars do not include power and status as an element in defining classes. This is due partly to the difficulty in measuring power and partly to the gradual elimination of aristocratic groups in these societies. The exclusion of power and status groups does not reduce the power of class analysis.[55]

In comparison, Mao's China was a unique society. The existence of three distinctive official status groups cut through occupational boundaries. Each status group was entitled to a certain amount of privileges and had its own distinctive social status and life style as defined by government regulations. Income, prestige and status were related to one another. For example, middle ranking cadres and professionals were in the middle of the income hierarchy and the prestige ladder.

Thus, the job ranking system produced a class structure, with high professionals and high cadres comprising the upper class; middle ranking professionals and cadres, the middle class; and junior cadres, low professionals, workers and peasants, the lower class.[56]

This classification coincides with the government definition of the high ranking, the middle ranking, and the low ranking cadres and professionals. In a sense, the status groups in the Mao era represented a classical example of the Weberian ideal type of classes in that economic classes and social status groups were nicely matched with each other.

Notes

1. Richard Kraus, *Class Conflict in Chinese Socialism* (New York: Columbia University Press, 1981).

2. State Statistical Bureau, *Fenjin de Sishinian, 1949-1989* (Forty Years of Progresses, 1949-1989) (Beijing: China Statistics Press, 1989), p. 448.

3. Statistical Bureau of Industry, Transportation, and Goods, *Zhongguo Gongye Jingji Tongji Ziliao 1949-1984* (Statistical Data of China's Industrial Economy, 1949-1984) (Beijing: China Statistics Press, 1985), Pp. 73 & 112.

4. Hong Yung Lee, *From Revolutionary Cadres to Party Technocrats in Socialist China* (Berkeley: University of California Press, 1991), p. 208.

5. State Statistical Bureau 1989 (footnote 2), p. 446.

6. Zhongguo Jiaoyu Nianjian Bianjibu, *Zhongguo Jiaoyu Nianjian, 1949-1981* (Yearbook of China's Education, 1949-1981) (Beijing: China Encyclopedia Press, 1984), p. 973.

7. State Statistical Bureau 1989 (footnote 2), p. 440.

8. Bernard Lewis Faber (ed.) *The Social Structure of East Europe* (New York: Praeger, 1976); Alex Inkeles, "Social Stratification and Mobility in the Soviet Union." *American Sociological Review* (1950) 15: Pp. 465-479; Richard Lowenthall, "Development vs. Utopia in Communist Policy." Pp. 33-116 in Chalmers Johnson (ed.) *Change in Communist Systems* (Stanford: Stanford University Press, 1970); Frank Perkin, *Class Inequality & Political Order* (New York: Praeger, 1971).

9. Inkeles 1950 (footnote 8); Johnson 1970 (footnote 8); Perkin 1971 (footnote 8).

10. Zhonggong Zhongyang Mao Zedong Xuanji Chuban Weiyuanhui, *Mao Zedong Xuanji Vol. 1* (Selected Works of Mao Zedong Vol. 1) (Beijing: People's Press, 1969), Pp. 83-93.

11. Cao Zhi, *Zhonghua Renmin Gongheguo Renshizhidu Gangyao* (An Outline of Personnel Management Policies of the PRC) (Beijing: Beijing University Press, 1985), Pp. 244-245, 260-266; Li, Guoying, *Shehui Zhuyi Gongzi Gailan* (An Outline of the Socialist Wage System) (Changchun: Jinlin Renmin Chubanshe, 1985).

12. Cao 1985 (footnote 11), Pp. 244-257; Li Weiyi, *Zhongguo Gongzi Zhidu* (Wage Systems in China) (Beijing: Zhongguo Laodong Chubanshe, 1991), Pp. 13, 27, 135-143.

13. Yao Shuben, *Sanshiwunian Zhigonggongzi Fazhan Gaishu* (An Outline of the Development of the Wage System in China for the Past 35 Years) (Beijing: Laodong Renshi Chubanshe, 1986), Pp. 13-38; Li 1991 (footnote 12), p. 27.

14. Cao 1985 (footnote 11), Pp. 258-259; Li 1991 (footnote 12), p. 143.

15. Kraus 1981 (footnote 1).

16. Cao 1985 (footnote 11), Pp. 267-302.

17. State Personnel Bureau, *Renshi Gongzuo Wenjian Xuanbian, Vol. II* (A Selection of Documents on Personnel Management in China, Vol. II) (Beijing: Laodong Renshi Chubanshe, 1986), Pp. 6-21; Cao 1985 (footnote 11), Pp. 267-302. Also see Yao 1986 (footnote 13).

18. Cao 1985 (footnote 11), Pp. 301-302; Yao 1986 (footnote 13), Pp. 124-132.

19. Cao 1985 (footnote 11), Pp. 302-308; 313-317; Li 1991 (footnote 12), Pp. 165-176; Yao 1986 (footnote 13).

20. State Personnel Bureau 1986 (footnote 17), Pp. 23-36. Also see Yao 1986 (footnote 13); Cao 1985 (footnote 11).

21. All dollar signs in this chapter refer to Chinese Yuan (*Renminbi*).

22. State Personnel Bureau 1986 (footnote 17), Pp. 6, 23. Also see Yao 1986 (footnote 13).

23. Yao 1986 (footnote 13), p. 193.

24. See Philip C. C. Huang, *The Peasant Family and Rural Development in the Yangzi Delta, 1350-1988* (Stanford: Stanford University Press, 1990), Pp. 174-185, 203-210; also see Anita Chan, Richard Madsen, and Jonathan Unger, *Chan Village* (Berkeley: University of California Press, 1984); Sulamith Potter and Jack M. Potter, *China's Peasants* (Cambridge and New York: Cambridge University Press, 1990); Vivienne Shue, *Peasant China in Transition* (Berkeley: University of California Press, 1980).

25. Andrew Walder, *Communist Neo-Traditionalism* (Berkeley: University of California Press, 1986); Yunxiang Yan, *The Flow of Gifts* (Stanford: Stanford University Press, 1996), p. 35.

26. Wang Kezhong et. al. *Dangdai Zhongguo de Zhigong Gongzi Fuli he Shehui Baoxian* (Wages, Benefits, and Social Security of State Workers in Contemporary China) (Beijing: Zhongguo Shehui Kexue Chubanshe, 1987), p. 166.

27. Randolph Barker and Radha Sinha (eds.), *The Chinese Agricultural Economy* (Boulder: Westview Press, 1982); John Burns, *Political Participation in Rural China* (Berkeley: University of California Press 1988); Nicolas Lardy, *Agriculture in China's Modern Economic Development* (Cambridge: Cambridge University Press, 1983), Chapter 4.

28. Kraus 1981 (footnote 1).

29. State Personnel Bureau 1986 (footnote 17), p. 6; Cao 1985 (footnote 11).

30. State Personnel Bureau 1986 (footnote 17), p. 15; Yao 1986 (footnote 13), p. 119.

31. State Personnel Bureau 1986 (footnote 17), p. 6; Yao 1986 (footnote 13), p. 119.

32. State Personnel Bureau 1986 (footnote 17), Pp. 6-9.

33. Yao 1986 (footnote 13), p. 119.

34. Yao 1986 (footnote 13), Pp. 140-157.

35. Personal observations and interviews.

36. After the wage adjustments in the 1960s and the 1970s, the average wage among state workers in 1979 reached $53.71. See The General Trade Union of China, *Zhongguo Zhigong Duiwu Zhuangkuang Diaocha* (The Status of the Labor Force in Industry) (Beijing: Gongren Chubanshe, 1986), p. 77.

37. Martin King Whyte and William L. Parish, *Urban Life in Contemporary China* (Chicago: University of Chicago Press, 1984), p. 32.

38. William L. Parish, "Destratification in China." Pp. 84-120 in James L. Watson (ed.) *Class and Social Stratification in Post-Revolution China* (Cambridge: Cambridge University Press, 1984).

39. Martin King Whyte, "Sexual Inequality under Socialism." Pp. 198-238 in Watson 1984 (footnote 38).

40. Yao 1986 (footnote 13), Pp. 13.

41. Interviews. Also see Cao 1985 (footnote 11), Pp. 246-247; Li 1991 (footnote 12), Pp. 135- 143; Yao 1986 (footnote 13), Pp. 13-21.

42. Personal observations and interviews. Also see Cao 1985 (footnote 11); Yao 1986 (footnote 13).

43. Personal observations and interviews.

44. Personal observations and interviews.

45. Personal observations and interviews.

46. Walter Connor, *Socialism, Politics, and Equality* (New York; Columbia University Press, 1979), p. 91; also see Alex Inkeles and Raymond Bauer, *The Soviet Citizen* (Cambridge: Harvard University Press, 1961); Alex Inkeles and Peter Rossi, "National Comparisons of Occupational Prestige." *American Journal of Sociology* (1956) 61: Pp. 329-339; Donald Treiman, *Occupational Prestige in Comparative Perspective* (New York: Academic press, 1977); Myrry Yanowitch and Wesley Fisher (eds) *Social Stratification and Mobility in the USSR* (White Plains, NY: International Arts and Sciences Press, 1973).

47. Susan Shirk, *Competitive Comrades* (Berkeley: University of California Press, 1982).

48. Zhang Xin-Xiang and Wang Han-Sheng, "China: Stratification in Transition." paper presented at the annual meeting of the American Sociological Association, 1992.

49. Nan Lin and Wen Xie, "Occupational Prestige in Urban China." *American Journal of Sociology* (January 1988) 93/4: Pp. 793-832; Lynn White, "A Leadership Diversifies." Pp. 67-113 in Victor Falkenheim (ed.) *Chinese Politics from Mao to Deng* (New York: Paragon House, 1989).

50. Lin and Xie 1988 (footnote 49); White 1989 (footnote 49).

51. Burns 1988 (footnote 27), p. 30; also see Sulamith Potter, "The Position of Peasants in Modern China's Social Order." *Modern China* (1983) 9/4: pp. 465-499.

52. Lin and Xie 1988 (footnote 49); Stella R. Quah et al. *Social Class in Singapore* (Singapore: Centre for Advanced Studies, National University of Singapore & Times Academic Press, 1991).

53. Elizabeth Croll, *The Politics of Marriage in Contemporary China* (Cambridge: Cambridge University Press, 1981).

54. Hans H. Gerth and C. W. Mills (eds.) *From Marx Weber* (New York: Oxford University Press, 1958).

55. Some studies of stratification in the US examine the impact of power, income, education and prestige on class formation and class relations. See John Dollard, *Caste and Class in a Southern Town* (New York: Doubley, Anchor Books, 1949); August B. Hollingshead, *Elmtown's Youth* (New York: John Wiley & Sons, 1949).

56. This was the basic criterion I used in categorizing the class positions of my informants' families.

4

CLASS AND CASTE

I have shown in Chapter 3 that stratification by occupational rank supplanted the old class system as a good guide to the socioeconomic position of individual Chinese in Mao's China. However, "class" designations and political role labels persisted as an officially structured carryover from the pre-1949 social relationships. Richard Kraus stresses that these two social hierarchies were abstractions and could not capture the rich complexity of social inequality in Mao's China. There was inequality in sex, age, geographical region, etc. Nevertheless, these two hierarchies were the most important dimensions of social stratification, constituting a key enabling us to understand the web of social relationships before and during the Cultural Revolution.[1]

Richard Kraus further points out that these two modes of stratification did not exist in isolation. They intertwined with each other and formed an important historical context within which a new set of social relationships emerged in China.[2] The most crucial aspect of the class system was its universal characteristic. People of both the upper and lower castes were represented within each class as defined by income, prestige and status. In other words, every Chinese was described simultaneously by both the caste hierarchy and class system.[3]

It is necessary to point out that these two scales measure different qualities. A person's position in one social hierarchy might not accord with his or her position as measured by the other. Before 1966, a person with a lower caste origin was not necessarily a member of the lower class. In fact, a substantial proportion of the upper and middle classes in the Mao era came from families with lower caste status. Several important historical factors contributed to the intertwining of class and caste.

The Communist Revolution

The interaction of class and caste in the Mao era occurred mainly because of the pre-1949 Communist Revolution. In essence, the Chinese Communist Movement was a peasant rebellion under the leadership of revolutionary intellectuals. Most of them were from exploiting class families that could afford their tuition and living expenses. They learned Marxism in school and ultimately joined the communist movement. They founded the Chinese Communist Party in 1921 and monopolized its leadership.[4]

Many middle ranking CCP cadres were also from non-revolutionary class families before the founding of the People's Republic of China. For example, in 1941, 42.8 percent of the CCP cadres at county level in the Jin-Cha-Ji Border areas were rich peasants, 42.8 percent were middle peasants, and only 14.4 percent were poor peasants. In 1940, 73.3 percent of county cadres in Beiye were intellectuals, whereas only 3.3 percent were workers, 1.1 percent were hired laborers, and 10 percent were poor peasants. The remaining 12.3 percent belonged to other occupational categories.[5]

Most cadres with poor peasant and other revolutionary class backgrounds were illiterate or semi-illiterate. They joined the communist revolution rather late and were found on the bottom rungs of the pre-1949 CCP hierarchy. In 1941, for example, 40.1 percent of the CCP cadres at village level in the Jin-Cha-Ji Border areas were poor peasants; 7.6 percent workers; 40.2 percent middle peasants; 6.7 percent rich peasants; 5.3 percent merchants; and 0.1 percent landlords.[6]

As another example, in 1940, in the communist border region in Beiye, 7.7 percent of the district cadres were workers; 6.5 percent hired laborers; 46.1 percent poor peasants; 17.54 percent middle peasants; 20.3 percent intellectuals; and 1.75 percent members of the "other class".[7]

The bias against workers and poor peasants in the CCP leadership recruitment persisted into the Mao era. Most leading cadres in post-1949 China continued to be founders and leaders of the pre-1949 Communist Revolution and were from non-proletarian origins. Among them were Mao Zedong (the son of a rich peasant), former Chairman of the CCP; Liu Shaoqi (the son of a landlord), former President of the People's Republic of China; Zhou Enlai (the grandson of a former Qing official), former Prime Minister of the PRC; Deng Xiaoping (the son of a landlord), former Secretary-General of the CCP; General Cheng Yi (the son of a landlord), former Foreign Minister of the PRC; Kang Shen (the son of a landlord), former member of the Standing Committee of the Politburo of the CCP, and still others.

As another example, the most powerful political organ in China is the Central Committee of the CCP. Franklin Houn identifies the family class backgrounds of 81 out of 97 members of the Eighth Central Committee of the CCP. Of the 81 Central Committee members, 28 were from landlord families; 23 from rich peasant families; 10 from well-to-do peasant families; 5 from official families; 4 from teacher families; 7 from working class families; and 4 from peasant families.[8] Robert North and Ithiel Pool report similar findings in their studies of Chinese communist elites.[9] Most of these leaders were in power between 1949 and 1966.[10]

Many middle ranking cadres in pre-1966 China were similarly from non-proletarian family backgrounds. Based on her study of 154 leading cadres at provincial, prefectural and county levels in Guangdong in 1950, Helen Siu reports that 1.94 percent of them were from working class families; 2.54 percent from handicraft worker families; 14.2 percent from poor peasant families; 35 percent from middle peasant families; 9.74 percent from rich peasant families; 18.8 percent from landlord families; 7.1 percent from petty capitalist families; and 10.78 percent from other types of class background.[11]

The vast majority of cadres with the "good class" background remained at the bottom of the power hierarchy in Mao's China. Helen Siu reports that in a sample of fifteen townships in Guangdong in 1952, 76 percent of the "key" township and village cadres and 78.1 percent of the "other" cadres were from peasant families. The sample further shows that 22.5 percent of the "key" cadres and 20.07 percent of the "other" cadres were from other types of families, and 1.23 percent of the "key" cadres and 1.2 percent of the "other" cadres were from landlord families or non-revolutionary families.[12]

Finally, tens of thousands of the Nationalist army officers and soldiers surrendered to the PLA during the Civil War of 1946-1949. Some joined the PLA, while others returned home. Those who had remained and been promoted in the PLA became part of the upper and middle classes in post-1949 China. For example, General Xu Huici, former Deputy Chief of the Staff-General of the PLA, had been a KMT soldier.[13] Those not joining the PLA and directly returning home instead became part of the lower caste lower class in Mao's China, despite the fact that most of them had been poor peasants before being enlisted by the pre-1949 Nationalist government.

Expertise

The CCP's need for expertise also contributed to the interaction of caste and class in the Mao era. China was a peasant society when the CCP rose to power in 1949. Most of professionals and intellectuals were from non-proletarian families and were in great demand. The CCP guaranteed their full employment in the state sector and paid them good salaries. Lynn White observes that a majority of technicians in Shanghai factories in 1963 were not members of working class families.[14]

The CCP also invited many former capitalists to manage state enterprises after the nationalization campaign in 1957. According to a 1978 survey of 6,123 former capitalists working in state enterprises in Shanghai, Tianjin and Wuxi, 2.99 percent of them were factory managers or directors, 15.24 percent heads of workshops or factory bureaus; 26.34 percent ordinary management personnel; 0.3 percent technicians; and 55.14 percent ordinary workers.[15]

The percentage of capitalists working in management positions (44.57 percent) was rather high. In 1980, only 9.7 percent of the total work force in Chinese industry were in management, whereas 84.5 percent were workers and service personnel.[16]

Education

The persistent strength of the bourgeoisie in the post-1949 social hierarchy was also shown in the inordinate number of its members in higher education and commerce,[17] a result of its historical control of cultural capital and business know-how. Most high and middle level intellectuals were from traditional well-to-do families and received their university education either in the West or in pre-1949 China.

Workers, poor peasants and other lower class people had to struggle for physical survival and were unable to provide higher education for their children. One of the grievances of Red Guards during the Cultural Revolution was the alleged monopoly of education by "capitalist academic authority figures" who had come from the lower caste (the "bad class") families.[18]

The CCP's "class" policy gave children of the "good class" preferential treatment in college admission and in application for the Communist Youth League membership. However, the implementation of the government "class" policy was not strictly observed before 1966. Most people were unaware of how exactly a person's family "class" origin affected his or her chances for higher education.

One respondent (Informant 49) said, "We did not pay attention to anyone's family class origin. I think at that time grades were the most important criterion for admission into senior high school or college. My family class background was not good. I entered a good secondary school because I excelled academically. So did several children of capitalists. Some children of workers did not do well academically and had to go to the countryside. Teachers were not interested in our family 'class' designations. They just wanted to send as many secondary school graduates to universities as possible. That was how the teachers got promoted."

As a matter of fact, few CCP leaders advocated a total abandonment of intellectual and professional standards in educational selection or job promotion. Most communist leaders readily understood the importance of expertise for China's industrialization, emphasizing that a revolutionary successor must be a "red" expert.

Thus, before 1963, university selection was largely based on academic records and college entrance examination scores. A good family class origin in itself was inadequate to assure success.[19] It was the children of the "bad class" families and professional families who excelled academically. A great deal of cultural capital was passed on from parents to children in these non-proletarian families.

Consequently, in competition for university education, children of the "bad class" families enjoyed a lot of advantages over children of the working class. It was estimated that approximately 3 percent of the "exploiting class" youth and only 0.5 percent of the "proletarian" youth attended college. As a matter of fact, the disparity was even greater than it appears in this estimate. Students from worker-peasant families were likely to attend inferior local colleges whereas children of urban intellectuals, the "bad class", and government officials attended major national universities,[20] who became middle class professionals after graduation.

After 1962 the CCP, under Mao's leadership, began to emphasize "class" struggle. Political behavior and "good" caste standing became increasingly important for college admission.[21] However, this policy did not prevent all "bad class" children from having a college education. More importantly, the class structure had already been developed since the introduction of the occupational ranking system in 1957.

The Interaction of Class and Caste

The interaction of class and caste created a complicated picture of social stratification in the Mao era. Although some lower caste people became middle class professionals and government officials in the pre-Cultural Revolution Chinese society, others were found at the bottom of the social hierarchy.[22] Many in the "good class" performed manual, unskilled jobs after the Communist Takeover in 1949, other "good class" people experienced unprecedented upward movement in employment and education.

In other words, the political status system did not preclude class differentiation within each caste. There was an upper class, middle class and lower class within each caste. Furthermore, as pointed out in Chapter 2, there were three castes in Mao's China: upper, middle and lower. Accordingly, Chinese society in the Mao era consisted of the following nine categories (Table 4.1).

1. an upper caste upper class,
2. an upper caste middle class,
3. an upper caste lower class,
4. a middle caste upper class,
5. a middle caste middle class,
6. a middle caste lower class,
7. a lower caste upper class,
8. a lower caste middle class,

9.   a lower caste lower class.

For example, if a cadre of grade four were from a worker's family, he would become part of the upper caste upper class. A grade three professor who was a member of a middle peasant family would be classified as a middle caste upper class individual. An engineer of grade two would be categorized as a lower caste upper class person if his father were a landlord. The same classification scheme applies to the remaining six categories.

TABLE 4.1 Class and Caste in Mao's China

	The upper caste	*The middle caste*	*The lower caste*
	(poor and lower middle peasants, workers, cadres, etc.)	(peddlers, middle peasants, etc.)	(former capitalists landlords, rightists "bad elements" etc.)
The upper class (cadres of grades 1-13, professors of grades 1-4, and their equivalents in other wage-grade systems, monthly salary: $135-$560	The upper caste upper class	The middle caste upper class	The lower caste upper class
The middle class (cadres of grade 14-17, college teachers of grades 5-9, and their equivalents in other wage-grade systems, monthly salary: $120-$80)	The upper caste middle class	The middle caste middle class	The lower caste middle class
The lower class (workers of grade 1-5, cadres of grades 18-30, and their equivalents in other wage-grade systems, monthly wages: $20-$70)	The upper caste lower class	The middle caste lower class	The lower caste lower class

In the following four chapters I show how class and caste formed an inseparable part of material and mental life, jointly affecting family life and adolescent behavior in the Mao era.[23]

Notes

1. Richard Kraus, *Class Conflict in Chinese Socialism* (New York: Columbia University Press, 1981).

2. Kraus 1981 (footnote 1).

3. Kraus 1981 (footnote 1), Pp. 35-38.

4. Donald Klein and John Israel, *Rebels and Bureaucrats: China's December 9ers* (Berkeley: University of California Press, 1976); John Israel, *Student Nationalism in China, 1927-1937* (Stanford: Hoover Institution Publications, 1966); Hong Yung Lee, *From Revolutionary Cadres to Party Technocrats in Socialist China* (Berkeley: University of California Press, 1991).

5. Lee 1991 (footnote 4), Pp. 31-33.

6. Lee 1991 (footnote 4), Pp. 31-33.

7. Lee 1991 (footnote 4), Pp. 31-33.

8. Franklin Houn, "The Eighth Central Committee of the Chinese Communist Party." *American Political Science Review* (June 1957) 51/2: Pp. 392-404.

9. Robert North and Ithiel Pool, *Kuomintang and Chinese Communist Elites* (Stanford: Stanford University Press, 1952).

10. See Robert Scalapino, "The Transition in Chinese Party Leadership." Pp. 67-148 in Robert Scalapino (ed.) *Elites in the People's Republic of China* (Seattle: University of Washington Press, 1972); Derek Waller, "The Evolution of the Chinese Communist Political Elites, 1931-1956." Pp. 41-66 in Robert Scalapino (ed.) *Elites in the People's Republic of China* (ed.) Robert Scalapino (Seattle: University of Washington Press, 1972).

11. Helen Siu, *Agents and Victims in South China* (New Haven: Yale University Press, 1989), p. 124.

12. Siu 1989 (footnote 11), Pp. 122-123, 125.

13. See Zhang Zhenglong, *Xuebai Xuehong* (Beijing: PLA Publishing House, 1989).

14. Lynn White, *Politics of Chaos* (Princeton: Princeton University Press, 1989), p. 183.

15. Library Section, The Institute of Philosophy, China Social Sciences Academy, *Sanshinian Jieji he Jiejidouzheng Lunwen Xuanji* (Selected Works on Class and Class Struggle for the Past 30 Years) (Beijing: China Social Sciences Academy, 1980), p. 693.

16. State Statistical Bureau, *Zhongguo Tongji Nianjian 1981* (China Statistical Yearbook 1981) (Hong Kong: Jingji Daobaoshe, 1982), p. 181.

17. Kraus 1981 (footnote 1), p. 80.

18. Kraus 1981 (footnote 1); Yen Chai-chi and Kao Kao, *The Ten Years History of the Chinese Cultural Revolution* (Taipei: Institute of Current China Studies, 1988).

19. Susan Shirk, *Competitive Comrades* (Berkeley: University of California Press, 1982), Pp. 15, 65, 71, 161; Jonathan Unger, *Education under Mao* (New York: Columbia University Press, 1982).

20. John Emerson, "Manpower Training and Utilization of Specialized Cadres, 1949-1968." Pp. 183-214 in John Lewis (ed.) *The City in Communist China* (Stanford: Stanford University Press, 1971); John Gardner, "Educated Youth and Urban-Rural Inequalities, 1958-1966." Pp. 235-286 in John Lewis (ed.) *The City in Communist China* (Stanford: Stanford University Press, 1971); Stanley Rosen, *Red Guard Factionalism*

and the Cultural Revolution in Guangzhou (Boulder: Westview Press, 1982); James Townsend, *The Revolutionization of Chinese Youth* (Berkeley: Center for Chinese Studies, University of California, 1967), Pp. 67-68.

21. David Radock, *Political Behavior of Adolescents in China* (Tucson: The University of Arizona Press, 1977); Shirk 1981 (footnote 19); Martin King Whyte and William L. Parish, *Urban Life in Contemporary China* (Chicago: University of Chicago Press, 1984).

22. Radock 1977 (footnote 21); Shirk 1981 (footnote 19); Whyte and Parish 1984 (footnote 21).

23. None of my informants was from the middle caste, the upper caste upper class, or the lower caste upper class. I thus focused in the book on the upper caste middle class, upper caste lower class, lower caste middle class, and lower caste lower class.

5

FAMILY LIFE AND POLITICAL BEHAVIOR IN PRE-1966 CHINA

I have described in the previous chapters the class system, the caste hierarchy and the interaction of class and caste in pre-1966 China. In this chapter, I compare middle class families with their lower class counterparts in the upper and lower castes respectively, examining the impacts of the post-1956 occupational ranking and political status on family life, educational achievements and patterns of behavioral development on the eve of the Cultural Revolution.

The Upper Caste

In pre-1966 China, workers, poor peasants, lower middle peasants, cadres, soldiers, and red experts were all designated as members of the upper caste and were in theory the "masters" of the state. Nevertheless, they belonged to different classes and did not enjoy the same amount of economic benefits and social privileges. The upper caste middle class families and their lower class counterparts experienced different life paths and exhibited different norms and political orientations.

Material Life

There are differences in material life between middle and lower class families in any society and so were there in Mao's China. Before the Cultural Revolution, the daily routine of most upper caste lower class children was to get up, eat, go to school, come back, eat again, go out to play, go home for dinner and finally go to bed. The Lunar Chinese New Year was an exception because the children could celebrate the holiday with fireworks and enjoy better meals. The regular daily diet of lower class families was simple, containing only meager amount of fish, meat and vegetables. Some lower class people were very poor and ate rice with salt or soy sauce regularly. Many male workers and peasants could only afford purchasing inexpensive low-quality liquor and cigarettes. Others consumed homemade tobacco products. Most lower class families had to prepare their budgets carefully for expenses on daily necessities, such as matches, soy sauce and salt. Lower class parents and children often wore clothes that had been mended many times. Their basic priority was food rather than clothing.

In contrast, many middle class parents could afford to outfit their children with new clothes each year. Nevertheless, middle class children liked to wear mended clothes to learn the traditional virtue of saving or to demonstrate revolutionary zeal. In Mao's China, wearing new clothes carried the risk of undermining a child's political future as this could be perceived as showing a desire for bourgeois lifestyles.

After 1962, the CCP asked Chinese people to learn from the People's Liberation Army. Many middle class children asked their parents for used PLA uniforms in order to display an enthusiastic response to the CCP's call. Lower class children wore old clothes as an economic necessity. Middle class children did so because it was a political show.

Middle class children frequently presented a rosy picture of family life in the pre-Cultural Revolution Chinese society. One middle class respondent (Informant 22) recalled: "Life before the Cultural Revolution was beautiful and tranquil. Weekends were my favorite. My parents often took me and my brother to dine out in restaurants. After the meals we went for a walk. There were many beautiful parks in Beijing. Trees looked peaceful. The blue sky! Sunshine! Fresh air! This idyllic-like life was broken into pieces when the Cultural Revolution took place all of a sudden in 1966."

Dining out at restaurants was a privilege that only people of the upper and middle classes could enjoy. Not all middle class families could afford frequent visits to restaurants. Some had several children and experienced a decline in living standards. Still, there were vegetables on their dinner tables. They were not limited to a diet of rice with soy sauce or salt as many lower class people were.

Most children of the middle class could afford lunch in school dining halls. They were spared having to go home for lunch and then return to school for the afternoon session. Children of the working class and junior cadres were denied this option, simply because they lacked the money. For lunch they had to go home and then to return to school for afternoon classes in all weather conditions.

Some middle class families had bicycles. A bicycle was a big-ticket item in the Mao era that lower class families could never be able to afford.

Middle class children realized the vast income difference between their families and those of the lower class. Many lower class children had applied for financial assistance from their schools because the monthly per capita income in their families had been $6 or even less.[1] The monthly per capita income among most middle class families was $25 or more. Middle class children did not think that their families were rich at all and wondered with amazement how lower class families could survive financially after all.

Housing

Middle class families and their lower class counterparts also differed in housing conditions. In the early 1950s, a substantial proportion of urban housing was privately owned. In 1955, for example, private home ownership stood for 53 percent of all housing units in Beijing and Tianjin; 60-70 percent in Shanghai and Nanjing; and 80 percent in Wuxi, Jiangsu Province.[2]

After the mid-1950s, urban landlords were forced to surrender their rental properties to the state. Individual homeowners were pressured to allow parts of their houses to be converted into multiple dwelling units to ease the overall housing shortage in urban China. New public housing estates were built by factories, government bureaus and urban housing offices. This process continued into the 1980s and resulted in a growing share of public housing in China's large cities. Martin King Whyte and William L. Parish estimate that by the mid-1970s, perhaps no more than 10 percent of housing in metropolises remained under private control.[3]

Public housing was very important to urban wage earners. They depended on wages for living and lacked purchasing power to buy houses. They lived either in public housing or in homes inherited from parents. Middle class families were more dependent on government housing than their lower class counterparts. Most high ranking and middle ranking cadres came from inland China after 1949 and were not native to cities of their residence. Nor were many high ranking and middle ranking intellectuals. University graduates were assigned jobs nationwide by the central government, in most cases away from their hometowns.

Workers and other lower class people were native to the cities where they lived and worked. Some of them shared housing with their parents and relatives. They could apply for public housing as well. Most people desired inexpensive public housing since it was heavily subsidized by the government. Generally, the government's housing policy favored middle class families.

William L. Parish reports, based on his Hong Kong interviews, that high professionals and government administrators fared no better than others in obtaining space and lodging for their families. But they were more fortunate in getting a kitchen, toilet and bath to themselves, for these often came with government quarters in which they were housed.[4]

Job ranking was a primary criterion for the distribution of public housing and for the quality of lodgings to which an individual was entitled. High officials and intellectuals and those holding middle positions in the state sector were more likely to get desirable public housing accommodations than were ordinary cadres, junior intellectuals and workers.

Generally speaking, the housing condition of middle class families was better than that of their lower class counterparts. One middle class respondent (Informant 45) once lived in a university's housing compound where the best houses went to professors; the next best to lecturers; and so on, down the occupational ranking hierarchy in the university. Workers, such as cooks, lived in basements.

Later, the informant moved to Tianjin and lived in a university flat with his uncle and grandmother. He found the social hierarchy there most impressive. He concluded that a residential segregation existed there, based exclusively on occupational ranking. Full professors lived in the West Village where the best housing was located; associate professors and lecturers resided in the North Village, the next best neighborhood; and workers lived in the East Village, the worst neighborhood. The informant wanted to become a professor on reaching adulthood so as to enjoy a big apartment in a good neighborhood. Other respondents told similar stories.

Child-Rearing Practices

Middle class families and lower class families adopt different child-rearing practices because of inequality in income and educational levels. In Western societies, middle class parents are better educated, enjoying social esteem and economic security. They use these advantages as positive sanctions for an effective molding of offspring in their own images.[5] Most of lower class parents lack such resources for motivating their children.

Middle class parents are also more likely than lower class parents to use reasoning, isolation of the child, and the threat of withdrawing parental love as means of disciplining their offspring. Lower class parents tend to adopt physical punishment in order to obtain children's compliance.[6]

Mao's China also exhibited salient differences in child-rearing between the middle and lower classes. Middle class families encouraged their children's mental development. Some middle class informants recalled their frequent tours to the Youth Palace to observe or participate in scientific experiments and other cultural events.

Middle class children read extensively. Several informants read books in their childhood that they were required to study in college later on. They had radios that allowed them to explore the outside world. Some middle class parents bought their children tools and components for assembling radios at home. Others subscribed to newspapers and popular science magazines for their children. Several middle class informants became interested in sciences after reading science fictions and *Ten Thousand Questions and Answers*.

Radios, newspapers and books were luxury items that lower class parents could not afford for their children. Many lower class parents had no access to newspapers and journals such as *The Red Flag*, even if they wanted to subscribe and had money enough to do so. Only CCP members were entitled to subscribe to *The Red Flag*.

Needless to say, there were no fancy books, Youth Palace or radios in the memories of lower class children. What they remembered most about their childhood was playing hide-and-seek and engaging in occasional street fights.

They also recalled that the best fighters in their schools and neighborhoods had been tough kids from lower class families. They however did not remember valuable family educational experience.

Finally, many middle class informants recalled that there had been a richly intellectual home environment that had encouraged literature critiques and constructive family discussions of politics. They reported that they had retained a strong interest in literature and politics since childhood. In contrast, there existed no such intellectual environment in lower class families.

Language

In the Mao era most high ranking and middle ranking cadres were from North China and spoke Mandarin. They held high prestige in society. Speaking Mandarin well helped raise one's status. A child who spoke Mandarin was often assumed to come from a cadre family.[7] In a sense this was a rather accurate predictor. Children of the middle class families were more likely to speak Mandarin than those of the lower class families. Mandarin, the official language, was also the language their parents spoke with them at home. Their parents were employed in government bureaus, schools, hospitals and other important state agencies where Mandarin was regularly used. Also the fact that many of their homes had radios added further to their children's exposure to Mandarin.

Most lower class parents had limited knowledge of Mandarin and speaking it was not essential to their employment. Unlike middle class children, lower class children had access to Mandarin only in school. They, commonly without radios at home, seldom heard Mandarin used since their parents and playmates conversed only in local dialects.

Academic Achievement

Many scholars point out that public education for the masses is claimed to promote a greater equality of opportunity. But study after study around the world has shown that children of educated urban elites, coming from literate families and with access to better schools, are consistently among the principal beneficiaries of the educational system. They persistently score better on examinations than children of the poor.[8]

Similarly, in Mao's China, children of government officials, party cadres and professionals were overly represented in urban "key" schools with the best teachers and teaching facilities. They were more likely than children of workers and peasants to finish high school, enter college and enjoy upward mobility.[9]

Many middle class respondents were well known in their schools for academic excellence. Often they won prizes in math, physics or composition competitions. In their memories, the vast majority of top students were from cadre or intellectual families.

Due to their higher academic achievement, middle class children were favored by their teachers and school leaders. Since academic study remained the focus of the school system, the institutional authorities were favorable toward students who best performed the institutional task. These students were from bourgeois families, cadre families and professional families.

Middle class children also benefited from the personal biases of many teachers. Because of the shortage of trained faculty, the government had to resort to teachers who themselves were more expert than "red". Julia Kwong reports that all of the 935,000 teachers in 1949 and the majority of the 3.5 million pedagogues in 1960 had received their education before 1949.[10] These teachers were biased against working class youth and preferred middle class students who were industrious, well mannered and nicely dressed.[11]

Furthermore, teachers were evaluated and promoted on the basis of the rate of success among their graduates in the competition for college admissions. Although admissions officially depended on the combination of political and academic criteria, teachers felt they could do more to improve their students' college entrance examination scores than they could to improve their students' political credentials.[12] Middle class children excelled academically and thus became teachers' pets.

In contrast, children of workers, peasants and peddlers usually attended the lower-quality schools and had fewer years of education.[13] Children of the working class families were often assigned to unskilled manual jobs after leaving school. When urban jobs became scarce in the 1960s, the government, in order to solve unemployment problems, sent secondary school graduates to the countryside. Children of the lower class families were the first ones to go.[14]

Occupational Aspirations

In the West, middle class children are more ambitious and have higher job expectations than lower class children.[15] Middle class children in China similarly aspired to higher occupational levels than their lower class counterparts did. They aimed to attend college and were never in doubt about their ability to fulfill their dreams. Their desired occupations were doctors, writers, researchers, scientists and university professors. Although they were eager to learn revolutionary virtues from workers and poor peasants, none of them recalled a desire to become a worker or peasant on reaching adulthood.

Lower class children did not hold any particular occupational ambitions. They did not expect to become persons of importance in the adult world. Although several lower class children attended elite graduate schools in the USA in the early 1990s, they argued that it was their "good luck" rather than their family training or childhood ambitions that had led them to their achievements. Since even these highly successful lower class offspring lacked childhood ambitions, it is quite easy to imagine how poor the childhood of other lower class children were under Mao's regime.

Values and Political Orientations

The differences among social strata are also marked by diverse norms, ideological orientations and political values. In the West, the high class tends not to emphasize manual labor, fighting, toughness, etc., all of which are valued by the lower class. The lower class children are less likely to appreciate intellectual values than their upper class counterparts. Middle class people are higher on the scale of political loyalty to the dominant ideology than lower class people. They are more likely than those below them to follow officially acceptable avenues leading to achievement of personal goals. These are principles which they depend on to reach their present positions.[16]

The positive association between class status and political orientations also existed in pre-1966 China. Middle class parents were very devoted to the socialist cause and often acquainted their children with the reasons why the CCP was great. One respondent (Informant 37) remembered that before the Cultural Revolution she seldom had talked to or played with her parents. She and her brother were usually in bed by the time her parents reached home. The children had latchkeys attached to neck rings and took care of themselves. Her parents often stressed that she and her brother should follow their teachers' instructions and study hard for communism. They wanted them both to become children of the CCP.

Family values have a significant impact on children's political orientation. Middle class children displayed emotional support for the socialist system. They believed that more than 75 percent of the people around the world had been waiting eagerly for liberation from colonialism, capitalism and imperialism. They wanted to be part of the revolutionary force to free working people from exploitation. They wished to join the PLA so that they could do what storybook war heroes had done. They hated the number one enemy of the Chinese Communist Revolution, Chiang Kai-shek, and American imperialism.

In comparison, the important values lower class parents taught their children were honesty, industriousness and kindness. Children of the upper caste lower class insisted that their parents had been workers or peasants and had not known much about politics.

Lower class families most certainly favored the communist government. The overwhelming majority of Chinese people were beneficiaries of the 1949 Communist Takeover. There was no reason for lower class parents to teach their children to be disloyal to the CCP. They nevertheless did not discuss politics with their children even though grateful to the CCP. They did not know much about politics since knowledge of politics was unnecessary in the performance of their jobs. The political environment in their homes was not conducive to the political socialization of their offspring.

Martin King Whyte discovers that in Mao's China workers and peasants were less likely than cadres or professionals to be socialized into politics or to be organized to participate in political activities.[17] During the highly politicized Cultural Revolution, many lower class parents still had a difficult time in understanding the basic facts of the Chinese Communist Revolution.

One respondent (Informant 12) attended a primary school during the Cultural Revolution. One day, his school invited a poor peasant to give students a lecture on the bitter life he had experienced prior to 1949. The peasant said that he had worked for a landlord. The landlord had given his family enough food to eat. During harvesting seasons the landlord had given him meat for his table. Life had become tough after the People's Commune was established. He then scolded the People's Commune and the government for their failures to take care of peasants in a 1961 famine, during which time many villagers died of hunger.[18] He concluded that Chairman Mao was now leading them to a new life.

As a matter of fact, the communist government established the People's Communes in 1958 and was in power when the 1961 famine occurred. The school wanted the poor peasant to glorify the CCP, but he ended up in berating the communist government instead.

It appears that there was emotional support for the communist regime among middle class families, while conformity to the socialist system was the dominant orientation among lower class families. The CCP would prefer turning all children into true believers of socialism. However, family background acted as a screening device to sort children into different categories leading to unequal socialization. Each social class has its own cultural practices by which its offspring learn distinctive values and behavior. Children of different social classes have different dispositions that influence their orientations and the way they react to dominant values and norms.

Political Activism

Andrew Walder points out that political activism (*Zhengzhi Biaoxian Jiji*, literally, "active political performance") was an individual's subjective quality evaluated continuously by his or her leaders and peers. In the Chinese factory system, the evaluation covered a person's work attitude, political thoughts, helpfulness to others, ability to maintain cordial relationships with others, willingness to obey leaders, eagerness to volunteer time for public work, readiness to criticize others' bad behavior, and the like.[19]

Similar considerations formed the basis of the political evaluation in the pre-1966 Chinese school. Teachers considered a child a political activist if he or she was academically excellent, obedient to his or her teachers, and willing to help his or her fellow students. Troublemakers and academic underachievers were viewed unfavorably by others as non-activists.[20]

Academic excellence, obedience and other "good" behavior were considered as the indicators of political activism because, in Mao's China, all such attributes were politicized. Before 1966, unless a student openly expressed his or her "selfish" intention to achieve upward mobility through higher education, his or her willingness to excel academically was not seen as a selfish career ambition. Rather, it was regarded as his or her enthusiastical response to the CCP's call to study hard for socialism. Similarly, when a student helped his or her classmates he or she was viewed not only as a kind person, but also as a person with a collective spirit who was always ready to fulfill his or her comradely responsibility.[21]

Generally speaking, middle class children were much more politically active than lower class children. They excelled academically, which was the most important hallmark of political activism. They did not have to spend as much time on studying as lower class children did and so had more time to volunteer for public work.

Additionally, middle class children had the ability and knowledge to help fellow students study, which helped them collect votes from lower class children in elections for leadership positions. They also needed to be politically active because they wanted to go to college. The official college admission policy demanded that candidates should have positive political evaluations from their teachers and fellow students.[22]

Many middle class children were student leaders because they excelled academically and volunteered for public work. They valued their elite status: college admission officials often used student leadership positions as an indicator of political activism. It was important for middle class children to be politically active.

Most lower class children were not political activists. They were academic underachievers and did not hold leadership positions in student organizations. Most of them needed help from others to finish homework. They did not expect to go to college and did not have to display activism to earn political credentials for college admission.

Other studies also show that in Mao's China political activism was most likely to occur in schools where the student body comprised mainly children of professionals and cadres. There was little activism in the schools that had a high proportion of youths from the working class and other lower classes.[23]

The Lower Caste

Class differentiation within the "bad class" created different life paths for lower caste children of different socioeconomic backgrounds in the pre-Cultural Revolution Chinese society. Martin King Whyte and William L. Parish compare the power of education with that of family political status and conclude that urban children were influenced not only by the "class" label that had marked their fathers' positions prior to 1949, but also by their fathers' current occupation and education. Children of well-educated fathers with low political status continued to do well in the occupational world.[24]

In contrast, people of the lower caste lower class were targeted by the CCP's "class struggle" policy. They were deprived socially and economically. People of the lower caste middle class differed greatly from those of the lower caste lower class in lifestyles and political behavior. The CCP's "class struggle" policy operated within the framework of the socioeconomic arrangement in the pre-1966 Chinese society.

Occupational Mobility and Caste Status

Diversity within the lower caste manifested itself first in social status. Before 1966 a family with a "bad class" origin did not necessarily fall to a low social standing. From time to time the government relied on post-1949 occupations to measure people's "class" status, which opened up the possibility to change one's "class" label (i.e., caste status) through occupational mobility.

For example, a member of a landlord family received a landlord "class" label by birth. His children also belonged to the "bad class" (the lower caste). If he joined the CCP and became a cadre, he would assume a "revolutionary cadre" label. His children then belonged to the "good class" (the upper caste). Many lower caste middle class people identified their caste status according to their occupations rather than their families' "bad class" connections. Such practice was widespread in urban areas where there was a great deal of occupational mobility.

The social position of the lower caste middle class was not challenged before the Cultural Revolution. Middle ranking cadres and professionals with a lower caste origin were in the middle of the income hierarchy. They enjoyed political power, financial security and occupational prestige as their upper caste counterparts did.

For example, the father of a respondent (Informant 47) was the son of a landlord but was quite safe politically before the Cultural Revolution. No one found fault with his family history. He was an associate professor in a college in Guangdong. Many teachers in the college were his former students. They respected him and were very friendly toward his family. The respondent and his brothers often went back to his father's home village for vacations. Peasants showed great respect for his father. "They asked their kids to play with us. We herded cows and went swimming with peasants' kids."

In contrast, landlords, rich peasants, "local despots", and former officials and soldiers of the pre-1949 Nationalist government were the primary targets of the land reforms and political campaigns in the 1950s and the 1960s. A few of them lost lives; while others survived the ordeals and sank into poverty and comprised the lower caste lower class. They and their offspring made a living in the countryside as peasants. In urban areas, most "bad elements" and rightists performed manual labor in neighborhood factories.

Unlike their middle class counterparts, these lowly placed people were unable to use their occupations to evade the political status system. They were identified by their "good class" neighbors as the "bad class" elements rather than as workers or peasants and suffered political prosecution before the Cultural Revolution.[25] The CCP exploited the lower caste lower class people as a negative example in political campaigns. The official discriminatory "class" policy had different meanings to the lower caste families of different classes. In the pre-1966 Chinese society, the class structure blurred the distinction between the lower caste and the upper caste for middle class people, but not for the lower caste lower class people.

Children of the Lower Caste

Children of the lower caste experienced different life chances, depending on their parents' occupations. Most children of the lower caste lower class had poor material life and were discriminated against in the labor market. They had no hope for upward mobility and disliked the socialist system. Susan Shirk reports that the children of the lower caste she studied had tended to be delinquents and were interested in finding boyfriends. They were without plans for the future.[26] In rural areas, male peasants with the lower caste background were discriminated against in the marriage market. Often, two lower caste families had to exchange brides with each other to ensure the marriages of their male offspring.[27]

Because of such bitter life experience, quite a few lower caste lower class children were alienated from the socialist regime. One lower caste lower class respondent (Informant 1) stated that he had lived with people at the bottom of society. "I saw how difficult life was in Mao's China. People struggled hard for survival. The communist government did not do anything nice for people like us, at least not to my knowledge. There were lots of injustices and unfairness in the pre-1966 Chinese society. In 1966 I went to Beijing and saw Chairman Mao Zedong in Tiananmen. All students around me jumped and cried happily. I did not feel the same way. I could not understand why they were so excited. I thought they were hysterical."

In contrast, children of the lower caste middle class were not viewed as social pariahs. It was their view that their family backgrounds were "cadres" or "professionals". They hardly differed from children of the upper caste middle class in terms of political orientations, life styles and childhood ambitions. Many of them were academic high achievers. They were political activists and leaders of student organizations. They expressed the same level of political loyalty toward Chairman Mao Zedong and the CCP as their upper caste middle class counterparts did.

A respondent from a lower caste middle class family (Informant 44) recalled his childhood: "My teachers liked me very much because I always got good grades and never caused trouble. I was not a student leader because I did not want to be one. My childhood dream was to become a writer, or a senior scientist, or a university professor. One day I toured the Beijing Observatory with my parents. I felt that everything in the Observatory was mysterious. The universe! The moon! The stars! Everything was very attractive. I then wanted to be an astronomer. Nevertheless, I still did not have a fixed goal. Any high professional job would do."

Class and Caste on the Eve of the Cultural Revolution

I have shown that life chances and political behavior in the pre-1966 Chinese society were patterned jointly by the class structure and the caste hierarchy. Consequently, there emerged two processes of childhood socialization in both the upper and lower castes. People of the upper caste middle class had higher income and tended to live in better housing, located in desirable neighborhoods. They were perceived by society as successful and received material and cultural benefits that led them to believe they were valued by the socialist system more highly than others. They were thus more active in politics and more likely to display an emotional attachment to the communist movement than people lower in the class hierarchy.

Children of the upper caste middle class and their lower class counterparts experienced different life chances. Unlike the lower class counterparts, middle class children were politically active and enjoyed leadership positions. Their elite status, their political activism, and their support to the communist regime were related to and reinforced with one another and created an elite mentality among them. They considered themselves revolutionary successors.

Similar class differentiation also occurred among the lower caste families. Children of the lower caste were socialized into various life paths and experienced different constraints and opportunities. The differentiating factor was the different family environments in which children of the lower caste grew up. They reacted to the social milieu in a variety of ways. Material life and emotional structures of the lower caste middle class families were more similar to those of the upper caste middle class families than to those of their lower caste lower class counterparts.

Of course this is not to say that the family political status system had no impact on behavioral development in the pre-1966 Chinese society. Many lower caste lower class people stayed at the bottom of the socioeconomic hierarchy in the Mao era and faced constant social discrimination. They reacted negatively to the socialist system.

Nevertheless, social standing in Mao's China was based not only on caste status but also on occupational ranking. The government "class" policy did not target the lower caste middle class people since they were identified mainly on the basis of their occupational status. Their political attitudes were influenced more by their class position than by their caste standing. The pre-1966 life experience of the children of different class and caste status had a great impact on their political behavior during the Cultural Revolution.

Notes

1. All the dollar signs in this chapter refer to Chinese yuan (Renminbi).

2. Su Xin, *Woguo Chengshi de Zhufang Wenti* (Urban Housing Problems in Our Country) (Beijing: China Social Sciences Press, 1987), p. 5.

3. Martin King Whyte and William L. Parish, *Urban Life in Contemporary China* (Chicago: University of Chicago Press, 1984), Pp. 81-82.

4. Willaim Parish, "Destratification in China." Pp. 84-120 in James L. Watson (ed.) *Class and Social Stratification in Post-Revolution China* (Cambridge: Cambridge University Press, 1984).

5. August Hollingshead, *Elmtown's Youth* (New York: John Wiley & Sons, Inc., 1949); Irving Krauss, *Stratification, Class, and Conflict* (New York: The Free Press, 1976); Thomas Lasswell, *Class and Stratum* (Boston: Houghton Mifflin Company 1965); Donald McKinley, *Social Class and Family Life* (Glencoe: The Free Press, 1963).

6. Hollingshead 1949 (footnote 5); Krauss 1976 (footnote 5); Lasswell 1965 (footnote 5); McKinley 1963 (footnote 5).

7. See Liang Heng and Judith Shapiro, *Son of the Revolution* (New York: Vintage, 1983).

8. Donald Munro, "Egalitarian Ideal and Educational Fact in Communist China." Pp. 256-301 in John Linbeck (ed.) *China: Management of A Revolutionary Society* (Seattle: University of Washington Press, 1971); Jonothan Unger, *Education under Mao* (New York: Columbia University Press, 1982).

9. Munro 1971 (footnote 8); Unger 1982 (footnote 8).

10. Julia Kwong, *The Cultural Revolution in China's School* (Stanford: Hoover Institution, 1988).

11. Kwong 1988 (footnote 10); also see Susan Shirk, *Competitive Comrades* (Berkeley: University of California Press, 1982); Unger 1982 (footnote 8).

12. Kwong 1988 (footnote 10); Shirk 1982 (footnote 11); Unger 1982 (footnote 8).

13. Shirk 1982 (footnote 11).

14. Thomas Bernstein, *Up to the Mountain and Down to the Village* (New Haven: Yale University Press, 1977); Peter Seybolt, *The Rustication of Urban Youth in China* (New York; M. E. Sharpe, 1977).

15. Stanley Coopersmith, *The Antecedents of Self-Esteem* (San Francisco: W. H. Freeman and Company, 1967); Alan Grey, *Class and Personality* (New York: International Publishers, 1969); Robert Hauser, *Socioeconomic Background and Educational Performance* (The Arnold and Caroline Rose Monograph Series in Sociology, American Sociology Association, 1971); Hollingshead 1949 (footnote 5); McKinley 1963 (footnote 5).

16. Urie Bronfenbrenner, "Socialization and Social Class through Space and Time." Pp. 400-425 in Eleanor E. Maccoby, Theodore Newcomber, and Engene L. Hartley (eds.) *Readings in Social Psychology* (New York: Henry Holt and Co., 1958); Glen H. Elder, "Role Relations, Socio-Cultural Environment and Autocratic Family Ideology." *Sociometry* (June 1965) 28: Pp. 173-96; Melvin Kohn, *Class and Conformity* (Chicago; University of Chicago Press, 1977); C. Richard Rehberg, Walder Schafer, and Judie Sinclair, "Adolescent Achievement Behavior, Family Authority Structure, and Parental Socialization Practices." *American Journal of Sociology* (May 1970) 75: Pp. 1012-1034;

62

Morris Rosenberg, *Society and the Adolescent Self-Image* (Princeton: Princeton University Press, 1972); Sidney Verba and Norman Nie, *Participation in America* (New York: Harper & Row, 1972).

17. Martin King Whyte, *Small Groups and Political Rituals in China* (Berkeley: University of California Press, 1974).

18. For information on China's Great Leap Famine of 1959-1961 see Dali L. Yang, *Calamity and Reform in China* (Stanford: Stanford University Press, 1996).

19. Andrew Walder, *Communist Neo-Traditionalism* (Berkeley: University of California Press, 1986), Pp. 132-135.

20. Interviews. Also see Anita Chan, Richard Madsen, and Jonathan Unger, "Students and Class Warfare: the Social Roots of the Red Guard Conflict in Guangzhou (Canton)." *The China Quarterly* (September 1980) no. 83: Pp. 397-446.

21. Interviews.

22. David Raddock, *Political Behavior of Adolescents in China* (Tucson: University of Arizona Press, 1977); Shirk 1982 (footnote 11); Unger 1982 (footnote 8).

23. Shirk 1982 (footnote 11).

24. Whyte and Parish 1984 (footnote 3), Pp. 50-51.

25. Lynn White, *Politics of Chaos* (Princeton: Princeton University Press, 1989), p. 11.

26. Raddock 1977 (footnote 22); Shirk 1982 (footnote 11); William L. Parish and Martin King Whyte, *Village and Family Life in Contemporary China* (Chicago: University of Chicago Press, 1978); Jonathan Unger, "The Class System in Rural China." Pp. 121-141 in Watson 1984 (footnote 4); Whyte and Parish 1984 (footnote 3).

27. Shirk 1982 (footnote 11).

28. Elizebath Croll, *The Politics of Marriage in Contemporary China* (Cambridge: Cambridge University Press, 1981); also see Anita Chan, Richard Madsen, and Jonathan Unger, *Chan Village* (Berkeley: University of California Press, 1984); Parish and White 1978 (footnote 26); Unger 1984 (footnote 26).

6

THE UPPER CASTE MIDDLE CLASS

Mao Zedong launched the Cultural Revolution to eliminate Liu Shaoqi and his supporters from the CCP. He also urged Red Guards and the masses to attack "bourgeois academic authority figures" and "white experts" in universities, research institutes, and state enterprises. Mao believed that high and middle intellectuals and professionals followed Liu Shaoqi enthusiastically before 1966 and should be taught a tough lesson.[1] With Mao's encouragement, Red Guards and "revolutionary rebels" attacked high ranking and middle ranking cadres and professionals ruthlessly. Government officials and the CCP cadres were hit equally hard by the Red Guard movement.[2]

Overnight, many upper and middle class people were deprived of political and economic rights and became social pariahs. Some of them were overwhelmed by the sudden deprivation. They committed suicide either as a last resort to escape social disgrace, or as a final attempt to defend their innocence and protest the social dislocation that they had regarded as utterly unjustified. After the initial shock, they began to search for adaptive options for satisfying basic needs and standards under the new circumstances.

In this chapter, I examine the Cultural Revolution experience of deprived upper caste middle class children, children whose parents were middle ranking cadres and professionals with the " good class" origin.

The Early Stage of the Cultural Revolution

Children of the upper caste middle class were very enthusiastic about the Cultural Revolution in its initial stage. They put up wall posters, struggled against their teachers and paraded the "five bad elements". Their schools were full of actions, excitements and fun.

More importantly, they regarded themselves the Red Guards of Chairman Mao and considered it their sacred mission to participate in the Cultural Revolution and defend socialism. They agreed with Mao's warning that the restoration of capitalism in China was imminent if they did not act immediately. They also believed that they would suffer if capitalism returned to China since they considered themselves future elite of the socialist state and part of the establishment. They asked: if they, the revolutionary successors, failed to fight for socialism, who else would?

Before the Cultural Revolution, many middle class children always regretted that they had not had the chance to fight the enemies of the Chinese Communist Revolution. They were not born then. Now they thought that the moment for them to defend socialism had finally arrived. They wanted to use their lives to protect the revolutionary cause which their parents had struggled for.

This revolutionary vanguardism reflected an elite mentality among middle class children. However, in the early stage of the Cultural Revolution, Red Guard detachments were formed by children of high ranking cadres and PLA generals. These detachments were socially exclusive organizations as they only accepted the applications from children of high ranking cadres.[3]

Since middle class parents were not high enough in the social hierarchy, their children were refused membership in the Red Guard. Middle class children felt humiliated and were outraged at the fact that they were disqualified simply because their parents were not high ranking party officials.

Later, in order to mobilize more people in the struggle against Liu Shaoqi and his followers, Mao's associates decreed that anyone could become a Red Guard if he or she was willing to fight for socialism.[4] Middle class children thus became eligible for joining existing Red Guard detachments or to form one of their own. Becoming a Red Guard was important for middle class children because it was an elite symbol. With a Red Guard armband, a child was socially recognized as entitled to engage in the revolution and to be a revolutionary successor, that is, to be a future master of the socialist state.

Family Deprivation

Middle class children considered it a revolution to struggle against their teachers and the "five bad elements". They enjoyed the Cultural Revolution very much until the day when Red Guards started to attack their parents. They were shocked. In their minds, their parents were "red experts" or loyal party cadres. They never expected their parents to be accused of being agents of capitalism. This was particularly true for children of the CCP cadres. They emphasized that their parents were true revolutionaries because they had joined the CCP before 1949 and thus should never be targets of the Cultural Revolution.

Children of middle class professionals were not certain whether their parents were as politically reliable as the CCP cadres. They however strongly believed that their parents supported the CCP and loved Chairman Mao Zedong. There was no way that their parents would do anything to undermine the socialist regime.

Thus, many upper caste middle class children were in a dilemma. On the one hand they had faith in Chairman Mao's policy of carrying out the Cultural

Revolution. They were against "capitalist roaders" and eager to defend Chinese socialism. On the other hand they rejected the accusation that their parents were "capitalist roaders" or "bourgeois academic authority figures". Believing that their parents were loyal supporters of the communist movement, they asserted that there would be extremely few good people in China if their parents were bad guys. They maintained that they did not form their opinions about their parents on the basis of family blood ties.

One upper caste middle class respondent (Informant 6) claimed that his father had led a guerrilla against the Nationalist army in a county in Sichuan in the 1940s. So his father had been a true revolutionary. He questioned the motive of the people who had joined the CCP after 1949. He labeled them opportunists because they enjoyed the fruits of the Communist Revolution without facing any risks. He stressed that people like his father had been prepared to die for the revolutionary cause. His father was struggled against and beaten up during the Cultural Revolution. In our 1990 interview, the respondent indicated that he was still unable to understand why his father had been targeted given that his father had not done any bad deeds.

Becoming a target of the Red Guard terror was a dangerous experience during the Cultural Revolution. Mao's associates sponsored the "revolutionary violence" against "capitalist roaders within the CCP" and "bourgeois academic authority figures". Many middle class people were subject to violent mass struggle meetings and beatings.[5] Several respondents recalled the sudden deaths of their family members, deaths which, according to their views, had been the result of physical abuse by the Red Guards.

Additionally, many middle class respondents reported that precious family possessions and furniture had been destroyed or confiscated by the Red Guards. The Red Guards also searched their apartments repeatedly for "evidence" against their parents. Many middle class parents were forced to dress up like clowns and were paraded in their work units and nearby communities for public entertainment.

Following public humiliation, many middle class families were ordered to surrender their nice apartments and move to low-income neighborhoods. Others were simply deported to the countryside to perform manual labor under the supervision of poor and lower middle peasants.

Significant income reduction was also a common experience of deprived middle class families. The Red Guards often arbitrarily withheld a large portion of the salaries of the middle class people, forcing middle class families to survive on a much smaller family budget. The worst scenario occurred when middle class parents were placed in detention centers, leaving their young children to take care of themselves.

Income reduction and physical abuse were accompanied by a loss of social status among middle class families. They had been in the middle of the social hierarchy and enjoyed occupational prestige before the Cultural Revolution. Suddenly, they were accused by the Red Guards of sabotaging the socialist system from within the CCP.[6] Middle class people, once labeled "capitalist roaders within the CCP" or "bourgeois academic authority figures", were seen in society as bad as the "five bad elements". Loss of family status had serious implications for middle class children.

Discrimination

Norman Denzin points out that the family sets the stage upon which a child's social identity is developed outside his home. He is defined by his family name, and the heritage of the family is his heritage. Sociologically, he is an inseparable part of it since he has not had an opportunity to emancipate himself from it and establish a station of his own in the prestige structure. When a child leaves his home and goes to the school, his family goes with him in a very real sense.[7]

Not surprisingly, children of deprived middle class families experienced severe social discrimination in school after their parents had been labeled "capitalist roaders" or "bourgeois academic authority figures". All of a sudden, all of their former friends pretended not to know them any more. They became socially isolated without anyone to play with. During the interviews, many informants recalled endless name-calling, intimidation, and physical abuse they had experienced during the Cultural Revolution. Lack of friendship, fear, and hostile environments both in school and in their neighborhoods were the frequent themes during my interviews with the children of the deprived middle class families. The experience was bitter because they thought that they had been unfairly treated in the same way as children of the "bad class".

One upper caste middle class respondent (Informant 40) recalled: "The son of a rich peasant and I were not allowed to join the 'Little Red Guard' organization and receive Chairman Mao's 'Little Red Book'. It hurt me very much. These students regarded me as a child of the 'bad class' and looked down upon me. How could they do that to me? I had been a student leader five months ago, had helped them study, and had recruited them into the 'Communist Little Pioneers'. They forgot my help just like that! Besides, my father was a cadre, not a 'bad classer'. It was unfair to treat me as a child of the 'bad class' people!"

Parental Adaptation

Deprivation produced a disparity between the past and present and thus became a stimulus among middle class families to search for adaptive responses to recover the loss. Concurrent with such adaptation efforts comes a psychological adjustment of attitudes, especially with reference to the conception of standards and social status of the family and family members. Status inconsistency fosters consciousness of self and others by evaluating the structure that defines the ways of social interaction.[8]

After losing their social status, many deprived middle class parents started to help their children adjust to the new environment. They tried their best to keep their children from knowing the truth. It is likely that they thought this line of adaptation could at least temporarily prevent the children from getting disoriented. In some instances the victims did not even tell their spouses about their political misfortunes.

The father of a middle class respondent (Informant 45) was struggled against at that time. His family knew he had been in trouble only after his aunt visited his factory. The aunt found out that the informant's father had been a key target of the political campaign during the previous three months. Wall posters condemning him were all over the factory.

Some deprived parents pursued other options to protect their children. Since it was impossible for the children to reestablish their positive identities in their hometowns, the parents sent them away to live in other cities. The children could assume a new social identity in the new environment.

Although middle class parents used different methods to protect their children, the ways they guided their children to adjust to deprivation psychologically were similar. Many of them told their children not to ask too many politically sensitive questions, emphasizing that the best thing for the children to do was to follow Chairman Mao's directives unconditionally. They said to their children that they were too young to understand the Cultural Revolution and their family problems.

Some upper caste middle class parents also said that the Cultural Revolution was timely, or capitalism might be restored in China. They did not blame the CCP or the Red Guards for their misfortunes, at least not in front of their children. Others told their children that the Red Guards struggled against them probably because they had unintentionally stood in the capitalist line and had thus become "capitalist roaders". The Cultural Revolution gave them a chance to return to the revolutionary camp.

Still, others maintained that they had not made any political mistake. They said that although they had been unfairly singled out and struggled against by the Red Guards, it was a good experience from a philosophical point of view. They were in fact given a valuable opportunity to think about the past and future and had benefited from such exercise. They would always be careful not to make any more mistakes so as to be in the correct political line in future.

Middle class parents also pointed out that it was inevitable to have some "minor" problems in a great mass movement. It was useless to remember past misunderstandings. What they needed to do was to look forward and raise their revolutionary consciousness.

For example, after the father of a middle class respondent (Informant 40) had been released from a "labor camp" by the Red Guards and was going to come back to power, many people came to congratulate her father upon his "good luck". The respondent recognized these people and hated them very much because she had seen them beating up her father in struggle meetings several months ago. When her father asked her to make tea for these people, she refused and walked away.

That night, her father had a long talk with her. He asked her not to be narrow-minded and not to blame these people for what they had done to him. Her father said that they were revolutionary masses, they were engaged in a revolution, after all. She was not able to understand why her father was so silly at that time.

It is difficult to know whether or not the upper caste middle class parents acted at that time. It is possible that they were unhappy but tried not to be negative in front of their children. Elizabeth Vaughan writes that during the Second World War, in a concentration camp run by the Japanese, adults deliberately pretended to hold certain ideas and values in order to make the children's life less wretched.[9]

Similarly, during the Cultural Revolution deprived middle class parents might try to keep their children out of depression psychologically by acting positively. They might also want to teach their children how to adjust to deprivation by playing the game with official rules. Their children indeed did so.

Children's Adaptation

In order to appreciate the consequences of status incongruity for children's adaptation, it is best to start with the occupant of a single status. Erving Goffman points out that the actor's position structures the expectations that others have of him, that he has of himself, and that he has regarding the appropriate behavior of others toward him. A stable social position, uncomplicated by the conflicting status, defines an expectable and routine situation. Social interaction is in general non-problematic, and self-identity reflects the integration and coherence of the social environment.[10]

However, when deprivation occurs, it places an individual in a state of status incongruity. Self-consciousness may be enhanced as the person seeks to adapt to threatening or fluid situations in which the actions, attitudes, and expectations of others are unknown or unpredictable.[11] The emergence of self-consciousness will sensitize the person to attitudes and expectations of others and act accordingly.

Such self-consciousness dictated children's adaptation patterns during the Cultural Revolution and generated two basic approaches: an "inward" approach and an "outward" approach. The "inward" approach focused on a child's efforts to build a new social identity by blaming his or her parents. The "outward" approach focused on a child's efforts to prove his or her social worth to the public by performing political activism.

The Inward Approach

It was not easy for middle class families to adjust to deprivation psychologically during the Cultural Revolution. There were no philosophical and moral grounds for a victim and his or her family to blame the CCP for the deprivation. The victim was accused of "walking the capitalist road within the CCP" or being "bourgeois academic authority figures". Blaming the CCP for the misfortune could only prove the validity of the verdict. There thus emerged a strong possibility for members of the household to blame the victim for family difficulties. Blaming the victim was conducive to family disintegration.

The tendency to blame the victim was encouraged by the CCP's policy toward the victim's family members. Studies of families under stress in the US show that the possibility for deprived families to dissolve is quite high if family members are offered a chance to leave the pressure area.[12]

Similarly, some deprived families experienced great family instability during the Cultural Revolution because the CCP allowed family members to escape the pressure area. In return, they had to display their "revolutionary consciousness" by dissociating themselves from the victim, showing that they placed loyalty to the CCP over that to their family member. The CCP saw this tactic as an effective means to break down the victim's resistance.

Consequently, some family members divorced victims; others participated in the persecution of their spouses; adult children publicly denounced their deprived parents. Such stories were a major theme of the "wound literature" swept over China after the Cultural Revolution.[13]

The very first novel of the "wound literature"—"The Wounds"—narrates a story of how an adolescent, after her mother, a party cadre, was accused of being a traitor, broke away from her family. She did not want to hear nor to believe her mother's defense. She went to the countryside, hoping to have her stigma removed and become a true revolutionary through hard manual labor.

In the countryside, the adolescent did not write to her mother nor went back for a visit until the day when she came to realize that her mother had been wrongly accused. She felt guilty and hurried home. She wanted to say sorry to her mother. But she never got the chance—her mother had died before she reached home. "The Wounds" caused a powerful echo in the post-Cultural Revolution Chinese society. Many middle class children saw their own images in "The Wounds".[14]

Most middle class respondents read and remembered "The Wounds". Some recalled a few incidences of the breakdowns of middle class families. However, none of them said that their own families had experienced such misfortunes. Nevertheless, some respondents were very happy to become "educated youth" despite the harsh living conditions in rural areas. They did not want to stay with their deprived parents at that time. Their social identities with their deprived parents became increasingly vague with the increase of the geographical distance between their parents and them.

Younger children did not have the choice to go to the countryside. They did not have resources to break away from their deprived parents. Dissociation from their parents would make their physical survival almost impossible. There were only two options for young children of deprived middle class families: (1) hoping that their parents had been wrongly accused and that their family political fortunes would be reversed once the misunderstandings were cleared up; or (2) urging their parents to confess to the revolutionary masses so that a possible pardon would be forthcoming.

The mother of one respondent (Informant 22) was charged with being a "bourgeois academic authority figure" and criticized by Red Guards in 1966. In 1967 his family was ordered to leave Beijing to live in a remote mountain area. His mother was again struggled against there. This time the accusation was more serious than the previous one. She was charged with attempting to overthrow Chairman Mao.

At that time he and his brother firmly believed that she was guilty because their teachers said so. Everyday when they came home from school they urged her to confess to the revolutionary masses, so that the masses would give her a chance to become a new person. Their teacher taught them what to say to their mother and they delivered the message to their mother. They hoped that she would become a new person soon.

The Outward Approach

Most deprived middle class children relied on the "outward approach" to manage deprivation. It was rather difficult for a child to carry out the "inward" approach due to emotional stress and limited financial resources. Further, there were conflicting official policies toward deprived families during the Cultural Revolution. On the one hand, children's status was related to that of their parents. On the other, the CCP decreed that the children did not have to break away from their parents to become revolutionaries, allowing them to build positive images despite their problematic family background. The "outward" approach was easier than the "inward" approach. All they needed to do was to perform political activism.[15]

Thus, many deprived middle class children focused their attention of adaptation on regaining public recognition for their revolutionary quality. Before the Cultural Revolution, their elite status was based primarily on their parents' occupational status, their leadership positions in student organizations, their academic performance and political activism. Now they had become part of the "bad class" and lost their student leadership positions. Academic performance was only marginally useful in establishing the eligibility for elite status in the politicized climate of the Cultural Revolution. Political activism became the only option available to them for retaining lost status.

Many upper caste middle class children said that they did not want to rely on other means (i.e., bribery, sexual favors, etc.) to regain their lost status. They claimed that they had known all these "dirty" tricks but had chosen not to use them. They did not like these methods and disliked the people who utilized them. They believed that a child with a correct proletarian ideology would certainly use political activism to claim elite status.

Being politically active was not difficult during the Cultural Revolution and was not very much different from that in the pre-1966 school. It included the following activities: volunteering time for public work, helping fellow students with their study, and being obedient to student leaders and teachers. These acts indicated a child's love for manual labor and his or her respect for discipline and authority. They also showed his or her "collective spirit" and "revolutionary feeling" toward his or her fellow students.

One respondent (Informant 12) reflected on his political activism during the Cultural Revolution:

"I spent my spare time cleaning our classroom. I helped publish wall newspapers. I also helped my teachers collect homework from students and marked them. It took me a great deal of time to finish these jobs. I worked hard when we went to the countryside to '*xuenong*' (to learn from poor and lower middle peasants). Students of the working class origin just played. They were lazy because they thought they were already very 'red' and did not have to work hard to prove their revolutionary quality. I believed that my efforts would be recognized eventually. My idea was proven wrong as my activism did not get recognized. My classmates never elected me as a student leader...I joined the 'Little Red Guard League' just before I left school. It was not glorious any more. By then everyone else had been a 'Little Red Guard' for some time. It was a joke, really."

Many deprived middle class children expressed a similar discontent over the fact that they had not been admitted into the "Little Red Guard League" or the "Communist Youth League" ahead of fellow students. They pointed out that the school authorities had to make sure that all secondary school graduates joined the "Little Red Guard League", otherwise it would represent the school authorities' failure in turning students into revolutionary successors. Therefore, it was in the school authorities' interest to see universal membership in the student organization. They claimed that this was the only reason why they had finally been admitted into the "Little Red Guard League".

Thus, the timing of entering the "Little Red Guard League" had significant political implications. Children who were regarded by the school authorities as "red" students joined the organization first, those considered backward elements, joined the "Little Red Guard League" last. Deprived middle class children concluded that the school authorities had refused to recognize their political activism since they had been allowed to join the "Little Red Guard League" last.

Not surprisingly, deprived middle class children were not grateful at all that they finally joined the "Little Red Guard League". They expressed displeasure at the school authorities because their primary goal of adaptation was to regain their lost status, not the mere acceptance.

Middle class children also complained that their classmates had not elected them as student leaders or the "five good students". Their classmates purposely overlooked numerous good deeds they had done for them. Their classmates also openly questioned their intention of being politically active. Other classmates claimed that they were only interested in personal gains.

Before children of deprived middle class families left school for the adult world, their parents had been released from "labor camps" and declared by Red Guards not guilty of being "capitalist roaders" or "bourgeois academic authority figures". But rehabilitation did not lead their parents to get their previous status back. Nor did it help middle class children regain lost status in school.

Furthermore, some deprived middle class parents were sent to the countryside together with their families to be educated by poor and lower middle peasants. Others stayed in their work units doing manual labor. Although they were no longer enemies of the people, they were not in a position to locate an urban job for their children. These legacies impinged upon the experience of children of deprived middle class families in the adult world.

Political Activism in the Adult World

When their parents were deprived socially during the Cultural Revolution, rebuilding a positive identity was a paramount concern among the deprived middle class children. They sought publicly to display their identifications with the official ideology, hoping to regain their lost status. Their endeavor often ended in failure.

The failure did not reduce their political activism in the adult world. Some of them found jobs in state factories, which was a privilege at that time. State enterprises and the PLA were the two institutions that provided economic security and social status during the Cultural Revolution. There should be no need or motivation for political activism among these middle class children.

Nevertheless, children of the upper caste middle class were still more likely to be "good" workers than others. They were habitual political activists. The workload in their factories was light and they did not have to work hard. No one dared to supervise workers who were considered the most revolutionary element in China at that time. Factory life was tedious and boring. Daily routines in work place did not provide a necessary background for political activism. Most workers liked to talk about their families, vegetable prices, and the like. When there were political campaigns, they read newspapers for about fifteen minutes, and then talked about something else. Generally speaking, workers did not discuss politics. If a worker tried to do so, others would think that he or she was phony and was eyeing for political gains.

Thus, many middle class respondents stated that they had not strived for political activism in work place. However, their leaders and coworkers often considered them political activists and rewarded them the honorable title—

"advanced workers". They were not politically active at that time, however. All they did was to run errands for workmates, helped factory leaders publish wall newspapers, and learned their trade. They thought that they had just done what they were supposed to do. They reckoned that to become an activist had been much less competitive in workplace than in school.

Political activism was kept very much alive among deprived middle class children who were unable to stay in cities. Urban factory jobs were scarce during the Cultural Revolution. According to government regulations, most secondary school graduates had to go to the countryside to be farmhands. Rural life was harsh: meals were barely edible; housing condition unbelievably terrible; and farm work physically demanding. Most people wanted to get an urban job and get away from the countryside as soon as possible.

However, during the Cultural Revolution, no one could simply return to his or her hometown to find a job. No educated youth was allowed to leave his or her village permanently without government permission. Further, the government controlled all urban jobs at that time. It recruited workers among the educated youths in rural areas from time to time. There were however not many recruitment drives and competitions were fierce. Displaying activism was important for "educated youths" to get a permit from the local government to return to urban areas.

Of course bribery and other illegitimate approaches could also get someone out of rural regions. Middle class children chose not to use them, considering them "incorrect wind" (*buzhengzhifeng,* inappropriate or illegitimate means) and labeling people who used them opportunists.

In rural areas, political activism was measured by a person's commitment to building the socialist countryside and willingness to be educated by poor and lower middle peasants. These measurements were rather vague. In reality, political activism meant nothing more than active participation in political campaigns, in addition to working harder and longer than others and being obedient to production team leaders.

Many middle class respondents agreed that after leaving senior high school they had no choice other than going to the countryside as "educated youths". They nevertheless stressed that they had been happy to go. They hoped to return to their hometowns after a few years in the countryside. They wanted to go to college or work in a state factory. They thought that they would still be happy to stay in the countryside, even if it were for a lifetime. They believed that they could do something to modernize rural areas. They had a "red heart". They worked hard in the countryside, although they did not know if they would ever be given a chance to go back to their hometowns.

Many upper caste middle class respondents also agreed that they had performed political activism in rural areas because they had wanted to use it to get out of the countryside. Nevertheless, they frequently cited revolutionary idealism as a major reason for their becoming educated youths and performing political activism in the countryside. The failure to get their revolutionary deeds recognized in school might generate a strong desire and determination among them to demonstrate political activism in rural areas.

One respondent (Informant 10) went to an "educated youth village" built by his father's factory. Educated youths there understood that they did not have to be politically active to go back to work in the factory. They were children of the workers in that factory, which would hire them back in two or three years. The respondent went to the village with revolutionary idealism, hoping to make a contribution to the socialist cause. He worked very hard and was responsible for putting up wall posters and presiding over other political activities. He was active not because he was after anything other than a public recognition of his revolutionary quality. His fellow educated youths in the village elected him as their head. The secretary of the local CCP branch urged him to apply for party membership.

Quite often children of the deprived middle class families went to rural areas with both revolutionary idealism and practical considerations. There was no conflict in these two orientations, which in fact might reinforce each other and contribute to political activism in the countryside.

In some other cases, middle class children went to the countryside and performed political activism purely because of their revolutionary idealism. For example, one respondent (Informant 7) did not have to go to the countryside. His elder sister was already an educated youth. According to official regulations, the government would assign him a job in his hometown. But at that time he was full of revolutionary idealism, wanting to be educated by poor and lower middle peasants through hard manual labor. He helped others and organized an entertainment team to propagandize the CCP's policy. He was elected a "model educated youth" and got to know many county leaders.

Some upper caste middle class children did not think about coming back to work in urban areas. All they had in mind was to be reformed by poor and lower middle peasants to become true revolutionary successors. They were not interested in staying in rich rural communities near their hometowns. They went to poor places such as Inner Mongolia, Heilongjiang, and Shaanxi instead. They longed for a harsh life in a grassland or in wildness. They believed that hardship would harden their "proletarian" spirits and purify their revolutionary quality. There were of course also traces of romantic imaginations deep in their minds about the grassland and wildness. Their revolutionary romanticism did not disappear until they fully tasted the harsh reality in rural regions.

In sum, revolutionary idealism was kept alive among children of the upper caste middle class and sustained their political activism in the adult world. They considered it their mission to contribute to Chinese socialism. They desired to be reformed by poor and lower middle peasants into true revolutionary successors. They always wanted to prove that they were more "red" than others.

Desocialization

Positive identification with an official ideology has a great impact on the way a person observes and interprets the external world. This is particularly true for children who are in the formative stage of political maturity. Ted Tapper points out that an official ideology is easily maintained in the classroom where social reality is modified (or distorted) to meet the ideology. Desocialization occurs most likely after children leave school as they will detect inconsistency between political messages that they learn from textbooks and social and economic realities they encounter in the real world.[16]

As can be expected, many children of the upper caste middle class experienced desocialization in the real world. In school, they were taught that Mao was a god-like hero who never made a mistake. Mao was believed to be always capable of carrying out revolutions successfully. The PLA soldiers, workers, and poor and lower middle peasants were said to have a broad vision of the world communist revolution and to be selfishless, courageous, collective oriented.

Mao's image broke down after the Lin Biao incident in 1971. Marshal Lin Biao was alleged to have engaged in a plot to assassinate Mao in 1971. When his attempt was aborted, Lin tried to escape to the Soviet Union but died in a plane crash in Mongolia.[17] When the news came, many middle class children were shocked. Their belief in Mao was shattered. They were not able to understand the "Lin Biao incident". If Mao were so great and never made a mistake, why would he choose Lin Biao as his successor? Their conclusion was that Mao was not that great. They no longer regarded Mao as a god and began to doubt the revolutionary cause Mao had advocated.

The wonderful image of workers and peasants that middle class children had learned in school disappeared soon after they entered the real world. Many middle class respondents were disappointed to discover that workers and peasants regarded work only as a means of making money, not as the means of contributing to socialism. Workers and peasants were simply not interested in the philosophical exploration of idealism, world revolutions, and communism.

Many middle class children also found out that daily conversations in workplaces were totally occupied by vegetable, meat, money, and women as well as naked, detailed description of sexual acts.

Worse yet, some upper caste middle class children were shocked to learn that some workers and poor and lower middle peasants missed the pre-1949 Chinese society very much. One respondent (Informant 29) always believed that poor peasants had been ruthlessly exploited by the landlord class before the 1949 liberation. She thought that they must hate the old society and love socialism. One day she went to work with a poor peasant. He told her that his material life had deteriorated after the 1949 liberation. In 1961 many villagers had died of hunger. She could not believe what she had heard. She even began to suspect that he was not a real poor peasant. Later, she heard similar stories from many other poor peasants and realized the low level of revolutionary class-consciousness among peasants.

In addition, many middle class respondents believed that peasants were selfish cowards. Middle class children witnessed abuses and injustices in rural areas. Many local cadres used their political power to rape women, embezzle public funds, and engage in other illegal activities. Peasants did not dare to do anything to these cadres. When the higher authorities sent down work teams to investigate the abuses, peasants did not dare to confront the guilty local leaders. Middle class children concluded that peasants had only known how to complain secretly and hoped that their neighbors would be stupid enough to step forward to face the powerful villain. So if the bad guy survived the challenge they would not face retaliation. Many middle class children developed a feeling of contempt toward peasants.

Finally, many middle class respondents claimed that peasants, including party members, had been very greedy. A respondent (Informant 7) said that one of his peasant friends had been in charge of the educated youth office in his commune. "Many other peasants were greedy and were not interested in politics. But he appeared different. He was a party member and kept making revolutionary statements in public. I truly believed that he was honest. In 1976 I was told that I had been chosen to work in a county factory. But this chance was almost ruined by that peasant. He gave me a hint to send him presents. I did not understand the hint because I did not think he would demand a bribe. He did not send my file to the county educated youth office. I almost missed the application deadline. Since then I began to distrust all peasants."

The image of the PLA soldiers was raised to an unprecedented high level at the beginning of the Cultural Revolution. Almost all middle class children said that at that time their dream had been to join the PLA. The PLA soldiers were said to be brave, selfishless, and loyal to the CCP and Chairman Mao. Many upper caste middle class children dreamed of having a PLA uniform and when they received one from their parents they were thrilled.

In 1967 Chairman Mao sent the PLA soldiers to take control of all levels of government to restore social order. The PLA soldiers were everywhere: they were in factories, schools, and government agencies. Once people got to know the PLA soldiers, they discovered that the PLA soldiers were nothing extraordinary. Many middle class children were disappointed to find out that the PLA soldiers were not smart, nor hygienic, and nor industrious at all. They also found that the PLA soldiers were rude, speaking foul languages all the time. They then decided that they would never join the PLA.

The elite mentality of the middle class children was based on the belief that they were revolutionary successors and the future masters of the socialist state. Their role models were the romantic images of Mao, the PLA soldiers, workers, and poor and lower middle peasants that they had learned from their textbooks. Now they lost their revolutionary conviction that had sustained their political activism. They did not know who revolutionaries were. They asserted that it was workers and poor and lower middle peasants who needed to be transformed into revolutionaries by them, not the other way around.

Children of the upper caste middle class also gradually realized the uselessness of political activism. In the real world, it was not political activism that counted. When government officials came to recruit "educated youths" to work in factories or go to college, it was personal connections, bribery, and sexual favors that determined the recruiters' decisions. No one cared much about political activism.

Furthermore, whenever there was a job recruitment drive, educated youths, no matter how friendly and helpful they had been to one another before, suddenly became hostile to each other. Everyone recommended himself or herself for the job and attacked others ruthlessly. There were lots of accusations and counteraccusations around. Many middle class children claimed that they had seen through human nature in the real world, had begun to distrust people, and had learned to become selfish. They maintained that they had just become "practical" and thus "mature".

This was not to say that they did not have career considerations previously. But now they gave up their revolutionary idealism and focused on their careers and personal interests. Some of them became disinterested in politics. They began to compare themselves with others in terms of success in career or other areas, but definitely not in terms of political activism as they would have done before leaving secondary school.

Others, though giving up their revolutionary idealism, believed that there had been social problems in China because a few bad guys occupied leadership positions in the government. They questioned the validity of the CCP's political propaganda but still sought to join the CCP. They thought that it was their duty to purify the CCP by eliminating the bad guys from it. They believed that this was the best way for them to contribute to socialism.

A small number of the upper caste middle class children thought that the socialist cause could be saved if there were legal and political reforms of the existing system. Immediately after the Cultural Revolution, some educated youths of the upper caste middle class origin returned to cities and participated in the "Beijing Spring" of 1978-1979.[18]

Interlude

Although the upper caste middle class was one of the main targets of the Cultural Revolution, not every middle class family was victimized. In fact, some middle class families stayed out of trouble throughout the traumatic era. It is difficult to estimate how many middle class families escaped the prosecution. It seems that only a minority of middle class families was free of trouble during the Cultural Revolution. Red Guards did not bother the upper caste middle class families under three very special circumstances.

First, the combination of several crucial factors: that the middle class people had no personal enemy around, that they had "good class" family origin, and that they were party members. For example, the father of a respondent (Informant 46) was not attacked by Red Guards during the Cultural Revolution. His father was on the CCP committee in his work unit and was from a poor peasant family. The respondent's grandpa was an old revolutionary guard. Finally, his father was very friendly toward everyone.

The second circumstance emerged when a cadre went to a new unit to work before the Cultural Revolution took place. The subordinates did not know him or her well enough. They had difficulties in collecting necessary information to struggle against him or her. Further, personal problems between the concerned parties had not developed yet.

For example, the father of a respondent (Informant 3) was not subject to mass criticism during the Cultural Revolution. He had been transferred to his unit two months before the Cultural Revolution occurred. Workers in that unit barely knew her father. In addition, her father was just demobilized from the PLA. In the early stage of the Cultural Revolution people respected the PLA soldiers. Her father's military service background certainly helped.

Finally, some military officers remained unharmed throughout the Cultural Revolution because Mao deliberately kept the PLA from being attacked by Red Guards.[19]

Children of the non-deprived middle class families did not have a good understanding of what was going on during the Cultural Revolution. They did not live in social disgrace resulting from deprivation, nor did they have a slightest idea about the adaptation that children of the deprived middle class families struggled so hard for. Although their family lives were not all rosy during the Cultural Revolution, they did not experience ups-and-downs as children of the deprived upper caste middle class did.

Non-deprivation did not produce family status change among these upper caste middle class children. It did not mean that they would not be politically active. They held leadership positions in student organizations and were "advanced elements". Their elite status demanded that they must be politically active.

Middle Class Children and Political Activism

The Cultural Revolution produced a status inconsistency among many upper caste middle class families as they experienced a downward movement in the social hierarchy in Mao's China. As Glen H. Elder points out, such situations tended to alter patterns of family and peer relationships, which was at odds with their normative expectations and customary norms. There therefore emerged comparisons between the immediate past and present in family socioeconomic status and in personal and public images of the family. Such comparisons were likely to create fear, discouragement, and family instability as present options were compared with previous patterns of social intercourse, and as the customary techniques of getting social recognition were proven no longer useful.[20] For example, academic excellence did not build up elite status in school for middle class children during the Cultural Revolution.

After the initial shock, deprived upper caste middle class children began to explore available options to restore their lost status. They experienced family deprivation not merely as a source of cognitive strain and emotional stress, but also as a powerful source of motivation for regaining their lost status. Their struggles were important because their previous social positions were highly valued. They also realized that the status loss was imposed rather than earned. They maintained hopes and a general commitment to the future during hard times. They struggled for social recognition instead of accepting the status loss passively.

Since their parents suffered political deprivation, children of the deprived upper caste middle class realized that their family background were a liability rather than an asset in promoting their social standing. In this context, family hardship might have increased the importance of personal efforts and merits. Children of the deprived upper caste middle class focused their adaptation efforts on political activism to prove or demonstrate their revolutionary consciousness. For them, political activism was a public statement of personal achievements and personal beliefs in Marxism and communism. They also hoped that it would function as a potential basis for status attainment.

Of course it is not true that status attainment could be reached only through political activism. During the Cultural Revolution there were many inappropriate but effective and popular devices, such as bribery, to achieve personal goals.[21] Nevertheless, children of the deprived upper caste middle class relied on political activism to adopt to the new situation, regarding it the only acceptable approach. They were aware of other alternatives. However, the family status loss did not coincide with the loss of their middle class values and behavioral patterns. They were politically active because they believed that only political activism built up a child's eligibility for elite status.

More importantly, upper caste middle class children adhered to political activism because the social conditions under which they had developed their social skills were defined by their class positions. Children were very likely to employ the family context and its values and behavioral patterns to judge and direct their social activities. Middle class children displayed emotional support to the socialist system and were politically active before the Cultural Revolution. It would be a big surprise if they suddenly abandoned political activism to strive for social status and job opportunities after 1966. As E. P. Thompson points out, people interpret the present from past experience.[22] They also use their customary norms and behavioral patterns to meet the new reality.

Notes

1. Lowell Dittmer, *Liu Shao-chi and the Chinese Cultural Revolution* (Berkeley: University of California Press, 1974); Harry Harding, *Organizing China* (Stanford: Stanford University Press, 1981); Harry Harding, *China's Second Revolution* (Washington DC: The Brooking Institute, 1989); Richard Kraus, *Pianos & Politics in China* (New York: Oxford University Press, 1989); Julia Kwong, *The Cultural Revolution in China's School* (Stanford: Hoover Institution Press, 1988); Yen Chai-chi and Kao Kao, *The Ten-Year History of the Chinese Cultural Revolution* (Taibei: Institute of Current China Studies, 1988); Xueguang Zhou and Liren Hou, "Children of the Cultural Revolution: The State and the Life Course in the People's Republic of China." *American Sociological Review* (1999) 64/1: Pp. 12-36.

2. Michael Frolic, *Mao's People* (Cambridge: Harvard University Press, 1980); Harding 1981 (footnote 1); Jing Lin, *The Red Guards' Path to Violence: Political, Educational, and Psychological Factors* (New York: Praeger, 1991); Anne Thurtson, "Victims of China's Cultural Revolution." Part 1, *Pacific Affairs* (Winter 1984/1985) 57: Pp. 599-620; Anne Thurtson, "Victims of China's Cultural Revolution." Part 2, *Pacific Affairs* (Spring 1985): Pp. 5-27; Anne Thurston, *Enemies of the People* (New York: Knopf, 1987); Anne Thurston, "Urban Violence during the Cultural Revolution." Pp.149-174 in Jonathan N. Lipman and Steven Harrell (eds.) *Violence in China* (Albany: State University of New York Press, 1990); Yen and Kao 1988 (footnote 1).

3. Gordon White, *The Politics of Class and Class Origin* (Contemporary China Centre, The Australian National University, 1974).

4. Yen and Kao 1988 (footnote 1).

5. Dittmer 1974 (footnote 1); Harding 1981 (footnote 1); Lin 1991 (footnote 2); Thurston 1987 (footnote 2); Thurston 1990 (footnote 2); Yen and Kao 1988 (footnote 1).

6. Dittmer 1974 (footnote 1); Harding 1981 (footnote 1); Lin 1991 (footnote 2); Thurston 1987 (footnote 2); Thurston 1990 (footnote 2); Yen and Kao 1988 (footnote 1).

7. Norman Denzin, *Childhood Socialization* (San Francisco: Jossey-Bass Publishers, 1977).

8. Glen H. Elder, *Children of the Great Depression* (Chicago: University of Chicago Press, 1974).

9. Elizabeth Vaughan, *Community under Stress* (Princeton: Princeton University Press, 1949).

10. Erving Goffman, *The Presentation of Self* (New York: Doubleday, 1959).

11. Alvin Gouldner and William Peterson, *Notes on Technology and the Moral Order* (Indianapolis: Bobbs-Merrill, 1961), p. 43.

12. Donald Hansen and Reuben Hill, "Families under Stress." Pp. 695-723 in Harold Christensen (ed.) *The Handbook of Marriage and the Family* (Chicago: Rand McNally, 1964).

13. Lu Xinhua et al., (trans. Geremie Marme and Bennett Lee) *The Wounded* (Hong Kong: Joint Publishing Company, 1979).

14. Lu 1979 (footnote 13).

15. Richard Kraus, *Class Conflict in Chinese Socialism* (New York: Columbia University Press, 1981); Jonothan Unger, *Education under Mao* (New York: Columbia University Press, 1982), p. 122; White 1974 (footnote 3).

16. Ted Tapper, *Political Education and Stability* (London: John Wiley, 1976).

17. See Chapter 3 for more information about Marshal Lin Biao.

18. Interviews. Also see Ruoxi Chen, *Democracy Wall and the Unofficial Journals* (Center for Chinese Studies, University of California, Berkeley, 1982); Andrew Nathan, *Chinese Democracy* (Berkeley: University of California Press, 1986); James Seymour, *The Fifth Modernization* (New York: Human Rights Publishing Groups, 1980).

19. Yen and Gao 1988 (footnote 1).

20. Elder 1974 (footnote 8).

21. See Andrew Walder, *Communist Neo-Traditionalism* (Berkeley: University of California Press, 1986).

22. E. P. Thompson, *The Making of the English Working Class* (New York: Vintage Books, 1966).

7

THE UPPER CASTE LOWER CLASS

Unlike their disgraced middle class counterparts, the upper caste lower class people were given social honor and opportunities for upward mobility during the Cultural Revolution. Chairman Mao Zedong and his associates declared that workers, poor peasants and other revolutionary masses were the backbone of the communist state, whereas high ranking and middle ranking intellectuals and cadres were the major targets of the Red Guard movement.

Mao's call was well received by lower ranking cadres, junior intellectuals, workers and poor peasants. They organized rebel organizations to struggle against "capitalist roaders within the CCP" and "bourgeois academic authority figures." Some upper caste lower class people rose to prominence and got into the most powerful political organization in China, the Central Committee of the CCP, during the Cultural Revolution.

Before 1966, all members of the CCP's Eighth Central Committee (1956-1969) were CCP cadres.[1] The Ninth Central Committee replaced the Eighth Central Committee in 1969. It was reported that out of the 170 full members of the Ninth Central Committee, 39 were workers and peasants; out of the 109 alternate members, 34 were workers and peasants.[2] Chen Yonggui, a peasant in the Dazai Production Brigade in Xiyang County, Shanxi Province, and Wu Guixian, a textile worker, entered the Politburo of the CCP, the inner circle of power in China.

Chairman Mao also ordered that at least one third of the executive board directors of every Revolutionary Committee in China, the ad hoc government during the Cultural Revolution, should be junior cadres, workers or poor and lower middle peasants, i.e., people of the upper caste lower class. They were invited to participate in the management of their enterprises or the People's Communes. They were also mobilized to take over schools.[3]

Despite their upward movement on the status ladder, most upper caste lower class families had to deal with many problems in everyday life. These problems were not the same as those faced by middle class families. Patterns of political participation among upper caste lower class people were also different from those of their middle class counterparts.

Political Involvement

Many scholars point out that the working class participation in the initial stage of the Cultural Revolution was marked by a political cleavage between permanent and temporary workers. The former tended to defend the political establishment and the latter to challenge the management in state enterprises.[4]

The root of this division seems to lie in their different socioeconomic positions in the Chinese factory system. Permanent workers enjoyed job security, medical benefits, good wages, retirement packages, subsidized public housing, as well as many other fringe benefits.[5] Temporary workers had none. Permanent workers commanded higher prestige than those who were temporary.[6] Clearly, socioeconomic differences among the different strata of the working class were reflected in the patterns of their participation in the Cultural Revolution, with material interests being the most important determinant of their political behavior.

It is also worth noting that upper caste lower class people participated in the Cultural Revolution not because they understood the theoretical importance of the Red Guard movement. Just because they were officially elevated in the ranks of prestige, did not mean that they reached a higher level of theoretical sophistication. As a matter of fact, they did not define a cadre as a capitalist roader according to Mao's "class" theory or official guidelines. They examined his or her concrete behavior instead. In their opinion, cadres were "capitalist roaders" if they had embezzled public funds, had taken bribes, had womanized or had engaged in other inappropriate conduct.

A lower class respondent (Informant 10) recalled that when the Cultural Revolution had spread to his parents' factory in 1966, many workers organized rebel detachments. A cadre in charge of the dining hall was given a beating by workers. They accused him of stealing their food rations and therefore "walking the capitalist road within the CCP". The CCP secretary of the factory was not similarly thrashed because workers considered him a good cadre. He had not demanded gifts or womanized. He had also helped workers whenever they had been in need.

After the initial involvement in the Cultural Revolution, most upper caste lower class people retreated into their private world and did not display initiatives in politics again. An upper caste lower class respondent (Informant 11) reported that at the beginning of the Cultural Revolution, workers in his father's factory posted numerous wall posters condemning some factory cadres, judging that they had distanced themselves from the masses and had not treated workers with respect and care.

Later on, the respondent himself became a worker in the same factory. By then many workers were no longer interested in political campaigns. Whenever there was a new political campaign, they just sat around and chatted among themselves. Andrew Walder's research on Chinese factories in the 1970s also demonstrates limited interests of state workers in politics.[7]

In rural regions many peasants were unaffected by the Cultural Revolution. Some villages were so remote from metropolitan areas that the political upheaval never reached them. Nothing extraordinary took place in these villages. There were no Red Guards, no "capitalist roaders", and no fighting. Peasants did farming and fishermen went fishing as usual. Most of them were illiterate or semi-illiterate with scant knowledge about the Cultural Revolution. In fact, they did not care much about national politics.

John P. Burns's study of political participation in rural China during the Cultural Revolution also shows the lack of political activism among peasants. He reports that the authorities in Fujian and Guangdong often had to pay peasants to attend village meetings. Peasants were generally inarticulate. Their interest was in free markets, private plots and small-scale commercial undertakings by families. Rural politics also involved struggles to protect the prestige of clans and neighborhoods. Peasants were unlikely to engage in political rhetoric.[8]

Like their parents, children of the upper caste lower class took part in the Cultural Revolution in its initial stage. Many of them joined Red Guard organizations. After the initial phase of the Cultural Revolution, they withdrew from politics. Sometimes, they sneaked away from their homes to enjoy flags, loud speakers, mass struggle meetings, the scenes of hitting "capitalist roaders" and the sight of endless throngs of people.

Interpreting the Cultural Revolution

Upper caste lower class children and their middle class counterparts gave different interpretations of the Cultural Revolution. Whenever the deprived middle class children talked about the Cultural Revolution, they recounted their family misfortunes and social discrimination they had suffered during the long period of social upheaval. Also, at the very outset of the political upheaval, they considered the Cultural Revolution a great and necessary social movement, one that would keep socialist China from becoming a capitalist country.

After their painful experience, they changed their minds. When they talked to me in the early 1990s, they regarded the Cultural Revolution as a terrible mistake committed by Mao and an unavoidable product of the "low cultural quality" of the Chinese people, asserting that Mao had been able to hoodwink the masses in the name of revolution. They suggested that there had been too many illiterate and semi-illiterate workers and peasants in China who had known nothing except worshiping "Emperor Mao".

Children of the upper caste lower class interpreted the Cultural Revolution from a totally different perspective. Instead of discussing theoretical implications and the importance of the Cultural Revolution for the world communist movement, they raised specific issues as the causes of the Cultural Revolution's occurrence, issues such as the abuse of power, corruption, and "deviant" lifestyles among cadres. They believed that the Cultural Revolution had taken place mainly because there had arisen an overabundance of social problems in society. Many cadres had looked after their own interests in preference to performing good deeds for ordinary people. These cadres had been ignorant toward workers and peasants. The upper caste lower class children asserted that good cadres and hard-working teachers had not been struggled against. Only those who had undergone problems were subject to mass criticism.

For example, a respondent (Informant 38) and his classmates struggled against a young female teacher, who had dressed up on weekends and gone out to dance with the school principal, a married man. To the respondent and his Red Guard comrades, such behavior was in the bourgeois lifestyle and totally unacceptable. The respondent agreed that the Cultural Revolution ended up in creating an excess of unwanted and negative outcomes. But he considered it highly inappropriate to negate the necessity of the Cultural Revolution just because of its bad ending.

Some lower class respondents asserted that the Cultural Revolution was not a revolutionary movement. Instead, it was just an opportunity for the feuds between different villages to perpetuate themselves, and thus an impetus for these villages to reinforce their mutual hatred. Other lower class respondents believed that clan politics were the biggest problem in China's rural areas. They claimed that rebel organizations in their home villages were formed on the basis of family surname lines and fought with one another. Mass campaigns were also waged against the interests of dominated clans. Small clans and non-locals were excluded from village politics and were socially discriminated against and economically exploited.

Daily Life

Upper caste lower class people did not have to prove their revolutionary consciousness as their "good class" background already granted them desirable social status. They did not strive for political activism for social recognition. They owed their social honor to their family status, something they just took for granted.

Thus, they did not treasure their inflated social status much. It came easily and did not give them concrete material benefits. When upper caste lower class children recalled childhood experience during the Cultural Revolution, they did not speak with gratitude about the absence of political deprivation. Nor did they talk about political activism, social recognization or desocialization. Instead, they discussed daily routines, the ill-equipped schools that they had attended and the need to work at an early age to help their families meet financial needs.

One respondent (Informant 38) recalled that his parents had never talked about politics with him. "They only knew farming. The only advice they gave to me was to be an honest person. They were not interested in the Cultural Revolution. I was in a secondary school then. I joined a Red Guard detachment to criticize some teachers...Six months later my father wrote to me, asking me to go back to work. I wanted to stay in school to have the glory of being a Red Guard. However, my family did not have the money. I had to return home to be a farmhand. Revolution was a nice thing. But I had to help my family first. I never got involved in politics after that."

Upper caste lower class respondents seldom aired any complaints against others. In contrast, their middle class counterparts often commented critically on their lower class counterparts. Middle class respondents did not think that working class children had shown impressive scholarship or revolutionary quality. They also asserted that they had volunteered to go to rural areas to display revolutionary idealism and to build a socialist countryside. But many upper caste lower class children did not respond to the government's policy. School leaders took turns to sit in the homes of these children everyday making their lives miserable so as to force them to go to the countryside.

Many middle class children felt puzzled and discontented. They argued that children of the working class should display proletarian consciousness and should do whatever the government asked them to do. After all, they were the offspring of the working class. Middle class children wondered why the working class children failed to possess the same enthusiasm for the CCP's call as they did.

Middle class children also complained that once working class children got urban factory jobs they were contented with their status quo. They did not want to learn trade or politics to upgrade themselves, neglecting to perform political activism. Middle class children asserted that most working class children were not future-oriented and were ordinary workers in terms of political performance and technical skills.

Nevertheless, middle class children agreed that most working class children were honest persons. They said that, if possible, working class children would have liked to get their job done.

Some middle class respondents went to the countryside as "educated youth" during the Cultural Revolution. Their evaluation of peasants was critical. While acknowledging that there were some nice rural folks, they complained that many peasants had not possessed revolutionary ideology, had not known anything about national politics, and had been extremely practical and greedy.

For example, many middle class respondents went to the countryside to learn how to become revolutionary successors. Peasants considered educated youths stupid to come to their villages to "suffer". Peasants were slow to follow national political campaigns. Occasionally peasants held meetings where they would shout, "Down with so-and-so!" despite the fact that they did not know who the "so-and-so" was. At times peasants fought with one another to settle scores that went back many years or even many generations ago.

Middle class respondents asserted that peasants exploited educated youths as cheap laborers. They assigned educated youths, male and female, heavy labor and did not care if a female educated youth might be in her menstrual period. Educated youths got fewer work points than female peasants. Peasants stole things from educated youths.

Many middle class respondents also pointed out that young male peasants were unbelievably lazy. Every day at 6.00 a.m. a team leader would raise them from their beds, getting them ready to go to work. Most of them did not reach the field till 9.00 a.m. When the workday ended, they would all scurry home. They did not work hard, spending much time on idle chatter. It was the female peasants who did the work. Many peasants frequently asked educated youth: "Want a wife? Let me help. Give me some gifts or a bottle of hard liquor or some money when you get married!"

Peasants also talked about money and sex. Worse yet, they discussed these topics in front of young female peasants. Some middle-aged female peasants joined the conversations with great interest. Many middle class respondents felt embarrassed and did not know how to react or what to say. They wondered why peasants never got tired of talking about such subjects.

This reflects the class difference between the upper caste middle class children and their lower class counterparts. Most workers and peasants were poor and illiterate and did not have the time, interest or energy to talk about national politics. They were interested in sensational fantasies rather than the world communist revolution since the subject of national politics was far removed from their daily lives. Sensational fantasies gave them temporary relief from boring daily struggles for meager subsistence. Social status, communism, Marxism and Mao's thought held only a modicum of meaning to them. Their primary concern was economic survival.

In my field interviews lower class children never took initiative to discuss the topics of daily conversations people of the lower class had. As their offspring, they were used to lower class languages and not surprised by the daily conversations of the lower class. They considered the talks too commonplace to be mentioned in the interviews. But when asked about these daily conversations they did not find fault with the descriptions of them given by middle class children.

Work

Most upper caste lower class children would drop out of school to work if jobs became available. Otherwise, they would finish secondary school and then go to the countryside as "educated youths" or "returning educated youths".[9] Work was very important because their families needed an extra income. However, they were not able to provide financial assistance to their families. They often went to the poorest countryside in the worst areas as they could not possibly compete with children of cadres and the PLA officers for going to rich villages.

"Educated youths" from the upper caste lower class families did not expect much chance of getting a job in urban areas. One middle class respondent (Informant 21) said that children from lower class families had comprised the overwhelming majority of his "educated youth village". After four years in the village, these "educated youths" became restless because no one had returned to his/her hometown. After the fifth year almost everybody was disappointed, angry and depressed.

The respondent stated, "They did not have money to buy alcohol to relieve themselves from depression. Nor did they have money to buy cigarettes. Not knowing what to do, they got irritated easily. Almost anything could provoke a fierce fight. It was scary. Some had premarital sex. When you came back from the field for a glass of water, you might see some people having sex, though they were not married. We all knew it and no one condemned such behavior. The fact of matter is that it was unacceptable for young people to have premarital sex in China at that time. I asked them to study and was happy to help them but they ignored me. So I studied myself. In 1977 when the government held a national college entrance examination, I was the only one in our 'educated youth village' to pass the exam and go to college. I did not know what happened to them after I left."

Not all upper caste lower class children went to the countryside. Some were allowed to stay in their hometowns. Also, the government had to give them a job. This was because their siblings had been educated youths. The official policy was that one family was allowed to keep one child at home and that the stay-at-home one should be given a job, either in a state factory or in an urban collective firm. These upper caste lower class children took the government policy for granted and expressed no gratitude to the CCP.

These upper caste lower class children usually received the least desirable job assignments. In most cases these were manual labor jobs. One respondent (Informant 12) went to a collective factory after leaving school. He was there because his father was a "capitalist roader". Other new workers were there because they came from workers' families. He did not consider it a big surprise as the parents of these workers did not have political power or connections to help them acquire better jobs.

Workers in that factory did not have social security and other benefits that workers in state factories enjoyed. Work in that factory was hard. Particularly in winter when they had to lift heavy objects from chilly water, subject to numerous painful cuts on their hands. There was no time for dallying or engaging in small talks since they were hired at piece-rate wages. Everyday work was physically demanding.

Some upper caste lower class children were very lucky to get good urban jobs. But they failed to see any connection between their "good luck" and the government. They just wanted to do their jobs and receive their wages. Having no political ambition for upward mobility, they were not interested in getting involved in politics. Their parents advised them to be obedient, to learn "real" skills and to be nice to other people. Their parents never asked them to become political activists.

In their parents' minds, politics was unimportant as it was just empty talk. When political campaigns were conducted they sat down passively to listen to activists without knowing what the activists were talking about. They simply did not pay any attention to the activists. They just wanted to be ordinary workers and be left alone.

It is not true that no upper caste lower class people played politics during the Cultural Revolution. Based on his study of Chinese workers in the 1970s, Andrew Walder reports that some activists were from the lower class background. They engaged in patron-client activities for opportunities of upward mobility. They curried favors from factory leaders and as a result were resented and isolated by their co-workers.[10] Judging from my interviews and Walder's work, it seems that the number of political activists with the lower class origin was small.

Immediately after the Cultural Revolution, some lower class children entered universities. They were unable to become sophisticated urbanites and be interested in politics at once. They considered themselves "country bumpkins". Their classmates would know that they were from the countryside by looking at their old-fashioned clothes or listening to their accent. They were not good at speaking in public. They just studied, studied and studied.

Lower Class Childhood and Politics

Economic conditions among lower class families severely limit options and resources and are known to foster apathy and restrict needs and goals.[11] Corresponding to their poor economic position, the upper caste lower class people were less likely to attach to official values and norms than their middle class counterparts. They enjoyed high social status during the Cultural Revolution. But that did not give them concrete material benefits. Social status was not a big deal to people whose primary concern was economic survival.

Children of the upper caste lower class were not heavily involved in the Red Guard Movement. Nor were they interested in the theoretical exploration of the importance of the Cultural Revolution. They were preoccupied with the need to assist their families. Unlike their upper caste middle class counterparts, they did not experience desocialization during the Cultural Revolution because they had not been socialized into political activism in the first place. They were not hard-pressed to strive for social status. In the context of their day-to-day economic problems, politics yielded them few desirable rewards. There were simply no economic incentives for them to be politically active. And their childhood was, after all, unrelated to politics.

Notes

1. Franklin Houn, "The Eighth Central Committee of the CCP." *American Political Science Review* (June 1957) 51/2: Pp. 392-404.

2. Donald W. Klein and Lois B. Hager, "The Ninth Central Committee." *The Chinese Quarterly* (January/March 1971) 45: Pp. 37-56.

3. Yen Chai-chi and Kao Kao, *The Ten-Year History of the Chinese Cultural Revolution* (Taibei: Institute of Current China Studies, 1988).

4. Alan Liu, *Political Culture and Group Conflict in Communist China* (Santa Barbara: Clio Books, 1976); Andrew Walder, *Communist Neo-Traditionalism* (Berkeley: University of California Press, 1986); Lynn White, *Politics of Chaos* (Princeton: Princeton University Press, 1989).

5. Walder 1986 (footnote 4).

6. Walder 1986 (footnote 4).

7. Walder 1986 (footnote 4).

8. John P. Burns, *Political Participation in Rural China* (Berkeley: University of California Press, 1988), Pp. 2, 11, & 68.

9. "Educated youths" held urban household registrations and were entitled theoretically to return to urban areas after a period of time in the countryside. "Returning educated youths" were children of peasants and had to stay in rural areas forever because they did not have urban household registrations. For information on the urban household registration system, see Tiejun Cheng and Mark Selden, "The Origins and Social Consequences of China's Hukou System." *The China Quarterly* (1994) no. 139: Pp. 644-668; Hein Mallee, "China's Household Registration System under Reform." *Development and Change* (1995) 26/1: Pp. 1-29; Mervyn Marthews, "Residence Controls in Present-Day China." *Asian Affairs* (1989) 20/2: Pp. 184-194.

10. Walder 1986 (footnote 4).

11. Glen Elder, *Children of the Great Depression* (Chicago: University of Chicago Press, 1974), p. 32; Melvin Kohn, *Class and Conformity* (Homewood: Dorsey 1977).

8

THE LOWER CASTE

The Cultural Revolution was a nightmare for lower caste families. The CCP expressed an unprecedented interest in the family political status of Chinese citizens during that traumatic period. "Class" origin and "class" struggle were stressed by Chairman Mao Zedong and his loyal followers.[1] If necessary, Red Guards would trace at any costs the family tree of a person to uncover his or her caste status. They would organize an investigation team going all the way to the person's hometown to retrieve information about the "class" background of his or her parents.

Thus, using ambiguous "class" labels to sidestep a person's real family political status identity became difficult and risky. Before 1966, some lower caste people in urban areas maintained that their caste label was "staff member" (*zhiyuan*) or "department store clerk" (*dianyuan*). It was revealed during the Cultural Revolution that these people's "class" label was actually "capitalist". They were punished accordingly for deceiving the government.

The Red Guards' interest in caste origins was motivated by the rationale that although the upper caste middle class people might have become "capitalist roaders within the CCP" or "bourgeois academic authority figures", they could be reformed as revolutionaries again because of their good caste standing. In contrast, the 1949 Communist victory took away the political and economic power of the exploiting class, people of the lower caste must loathe the socialist regime and were reactionaries by nature.

As a matter of fact, before 1966, the CCP already carried out the "class struggle" policy against the "five bad elements" (people of the lower caste lower class) as mentioned in Chapter 5. What is unique about the Cultural Revolution was the Red Guards' interest in the "class" origins of the lower caste middle class people. The Red Guards believed that the lower caste middle class people had "disguized" themselves as revolutionaries or academic authority figures. The Red Guards asserted that because of their official posts in the civil service and the education sector, the lower caste middle class people were in a good position to reclaim their "class" power and privileges and to restore capitalism in China. To the Red Guards, family political status counted for everything, occupational standing did not.

Consequently, virtually all lower caste families, regardless of class position, lived under the Red Guard terror. Nevertheless, deprivation had different meanings to families of different socioeconomic status and resources. This in turn led these families to devise a variety of adaptive strategies to manage the stress generated by the Cultural Revolution.

Deprivation of the Lower Caste Families: the Lower Class Experience

Families of the lower caste lower class had been subject to severe social discrimination long before the Cultural Revolution occurred in 1966.[2] Living in a persistently oppressive environment tended to foster among these families habitual submission to discrimination. Studies of caste societies show that when lower caste lower class individuals are abused by people of the upper caste, they do not seek to resist or retaliate in order to redress their grievances. They learn from bitter experience that passive acceptance is the best and often the only solution to avoid greater harm.[3]

Not surprisingly, most lower caste lower class people used non-resistance as a major adaptive device during the Cultural Revolution. Quite a few of them lost jobs after 1966 simply because of their "bad class" connections. They had no choice but to accept their fates.

In both cities and rural areas people of the lower caste lower class were ordered to clean public toilets or do other community work. Each time a political campaign took place, they had to submit self-confessions to the local government. Without resisting, they did what they were told. Anyone could physically abuse them or order them to do their bidding. These lowly placed people and their children maintained a low profile and did their utmost to avoid arguments with others.

One "good class" respondent (Informant 32) often taunted his neighbor, a landlord's grandson, during the Cultural Revolution. They were about the same size and age. Sometimes the respondent managed to give his opponent a beating. On other occasions the landlord's grandson got the upper hand. Then the respondent would yell "you son of a landlord". The landlord's grandson would run away immediately. The respondent favored this tactic because it was so effective. Each time he used it he won the encounter.

Jonathan Unger reports that some peasant "bad class" descendants grew up burdened by confused feelings of inferiority. A peasant recalls that even as a small child, "I didn't quarrel much. People called me 'landlord son'. I felt inferior, hopeless, as if things were beyond my control. It was so unfair. Take me, I was born after the peace...Even if my parents had done something wrong, exploited other people, why should I be discriminated against? I felt inferior, never dared to do anything. Even before I got involved in any quarrel, I'd already say to myself: 'Eh, the only thing I can do is to live with my head down.' Usually at school the teachers treated me like any other kid. But if I did something wrong and got a scolding, they'd bring out my class background: 'You mean you side with your parents rather than the poor-and-lower-middle peasants?!'"[4]

Children of the lower caste lower class were rich in experiencing social discrimination but poor in resources to cope with difficult situations. Some "educated youths" went to farm in rural areas for a few years and then returned to work in cities. Many others stayed in the countryside but kept alive their hopes of going back to their hometowns.

However, there were no hopes for "educated youths" with the lower caste lower class origin. They knew that the government meant to settle them in rural regions for a lifetime. Many respondents observed that these educated youths worked very hard and were honest and warm-hearted. But because of their lower caste lower class family background, no one wanted to help them out. They were also very poor. Quite often their only diet was rice with salt. They could not afford to send gifts to village leaders. Gifts however were crucial for a person to get a permit and letter of reference from the village leaders to apply for university education or an urban job.

Neither did lower caste lower class families have reliable network resources to solve their problems. Having been the target of the CCP's "class" struggle policy since the early 1950s, they had become social isolates in their neighborhoods. Most people, including their relatives and friends, avoided contracts with them and in no way would these people risk their political life to help them.

Occasionally, out of desperation, some lower caste lower class children confronted children of the upper caste. This approach was futile under the Red Guard terror. One respondent (Informant 54) had a classmate whose grandfather had been a landlord. Whenever this classmate argued with other students, they would yell "son of a landlord" at him. Becoming extremely angry and red-faced, he would then fight with these upper caste children. The upper caste students would then rush to inform their teachers by whom he would then be reprimanded.

Another lower caste respondent (Informant 51) recalled that some Red Guards had come to her home once and had ordered her family to relocate to a remote area in Shende County in Guangdong. "My grandma quarreled with the Red Guards. She said that she would not go anywhere. Her home was here and unless they killed her she would remain here. In addition, none of her grandchildren would go elsewhere. The Red Guards were very angry and kept coming back to struggle against my grandmother for about a month."

Deprivation of the Lower Caste Families: the Middle Class Experience

Before 1966 families of the lower caste middle class were placed in the middle of the socioeconomic hierarchy and thus did not experience caste discrimination. However, during the Cultural Revolution, they lost the immunity from political discrimination that they had previously enjoyed. Chairman Mao Zedong insisted that politics should take command in China. The technical expertise of professionals of the lower caste was no longer needed. Nor could CCP cadres with the lower caste connections escape political prosecution. During the Cultural Revolution, positions in the government bureaucracy were a liability rather than an asset in maintaining a desirable status.

Thus, for the first time, families of the lower caste middle class tasted the bitterness of caste discrimination that their lower class counterparts had long experienced. Because of their lower caste connections, lower caste middle class people were labeled not only as "bourgeois academic authority figures" or "capitalist roaders", but also as "sons/daughters of landlords/capitalists" and "historical reactionaries".

Like their upper caste counterparts, lower caste middle class parents were subject to violent mass struggle meetings, demotions and income reductions during the Cultural Revolution. Some of them were banished to the countryside to perform manual labor. To families of the lower caste middle class, deprivation seemed unbearable and painful, serving as a powerful stimulus for them to adapt to adversity.

Deprivation Experience

With the downfall of their parents, children of the lower caste middle class lost their elite status and became the "real" offspring of the lower caste. They had difficulty adjusting to the new reality. Before the social upheaval, they took it for granted that their "class" origins were those of their parents' occupations: cadres, managers, engineers, professors, etc. They did not know that their families belonged to the lower caste. Their parents deliberately withheld their family's history from them since there was nothing to be gained by revealing it.

During the Cultural Revolution, political deprivation forced them to abandon customary perceptions of their families' social status, demanding that they view themselves as the children of the lower caste. Accepting the lower caste identity was hard on them. Adapting to this psychological transition and behavioral adjustment proved to be an equally tough battle.

A respondent (Informant 21) recalled: "One day my father came home with a big sign in front of his chest, identifying him as a 'black element.' I was shocked. How could this be possible? My father was a communist party member and an associate professor...My father told us that he was the son of a landlord. What!? I kept asking myself, 'Why me? Why was my lot so bitter?'"

Although children of the lower caste middle class understood that they could no loner assume the upper caste status, they still resented very much that their teachers and classmates treated them as children of the lower caste. Their reaction to this undesirable and drastic downgrade in status was denial. They made no attempt to reconcile the conflict between reality and their customary perceptions. They insisted that only people of the lower caste lower class had been the real "bad classers".

Thus, lower caste middle class children possessed a strong curiosity about the lower caste people and kept "revolutionary vigilance" against these people when they went to the countryside or factories to work. They were surprised to discover that many "bad class" people were just like ordinary people, who did not exhibit the features of the "ghost and demon".

For example, the father of a lower caste middle class respondent (Informant 13) was unfortunately labeled a "rightist" in 1957. Her mother had to divorce him to protect herself politically. Her stepfather was a writer and was from a landlord family. Being a child of the lower caste herself, she remembered her "first" encounter with people of the "real" lower caste:

"Before I went to the countryside as an educated youth, I had known something about people of the 'bad class' from textbooks. I reckoned that before the 1949 liberation, people of the 'bad class' must have dressed in silk, have eaten delicious food everyday, and have exploited poor peasants ruthlessly. They were bad guys. After I became an educated youth in a village, I was interested in 'class struggle' there. I wanted to find out who people of the 'bad class' were. The villagers told me that they had only one landlord there. I asked, 'Was he a cold-blooded exploiter before 1949? Was he very rich? Does he hate socialism? Do poor peasants keep an eye on him?'"

"The villagers thought that my questions were funny and laughed at me. They said the landlord actually did not own a lot of land before 1949. In the land reform of 1950-1952, officials from the government land reform work team insisted on labeling someone 'landlord' in their village. The richest farmer in the village was unfortunately picked out. I nevertheless was still very curious about the landlord. Later I got a chance to talk to him privately and found out that he was quite a nice person."

Although the lower caste middle class children realized that everything they saw in the real world was different from textbook depictions, they still distanced themselves from people of the lower caste lower class, thus making a public statement that by no means were they related to these people. They accepted the prejudice of the majority society against people of the "bad class", agreeing that discrimination against people of the lower caste lower class was justifiable. They still acted as if they were revolutionary successors. Unfortunately, their classmates and teachers did not agree with that and treated them as the offspring of the lower caste.

One respondent (Informant 47) recalled that when the Cultural Revolution occurred, "my father, an associate professor, was labeled as a "historical reactionary" because he was the son of a landlord. He was laid off and our family was sent back to his home village. Formerly friendly peasants suddenly became hostile toward us. My brothers and I however still wanted to defend Chairman Mao and socialism. We still thought that we were somebody. We organized a Red Guard detachment to rebel against leaders of the production brigade in the village. Three months later, we were ordered to disband our detachment and were labeled 'current reactionaries'. The production brigade leaders said that because of our problematic family background we were disqualified to carry out the revolution. I was forced to confess my 'crimes' in a detention center. Later, a deputy head of our production brigade ordered me to work with the 'five bad elements' and their children. I was stunned and angry. They made me work with the 'five bad elements'!"

Another lower caste middle class respondent (Informant 21) was a student leader before the Cultural Revolution, liked by many teachers for his academic excellence. When his father, an associate professor in a local college, was assailed at the outset of the Cultural Revolution for his landlord family connection, he became a child of the "bad class" instantly.

One day in 1967 he was arrested by school authorities and charged with writing an anti-Mao Zedong slogan on the wall of an abandoned house the day before. This was a serious crime and could lead to a death sentence. He had been at the house that day but had not written anything there. Even though other kids had been at the scene as well, he was singled out solely because of his family class origin.

Released eight months later, he was told that the school authorities had failed to match his handwriting with that of the slogan writer as early as two weeks following his arrest. Still, school officials kept interrogating and hitting him. His brother, who had not even been on the scene that day, was arrested on the same charge. Authorities held his brother captive until he was driven insane.

Because life was difficult for the lower caste people, children of the lower caste middle class refused to view their families as those of the "bad class" during the Cultural Revolution. Surprisingly, this attitude was still held firmly when I interviewed them in the early 1990s. As a matter of fact, the CCP officially abolished the political status system in 1979. A "bad class" connection no longer sounds demeaning today as it did in Mao's China.

Nevertheless, during the interviews, children of the lower caste middle class still insisted that their families were of the revolutionary origin, rejecting the suggestion that they belonged to the "bad class". Many of them claimed that their grandparents had been good persons and in fact had little land or capital, emphasizing that their grandparents were different from the lower caste lower class people. They blamed government officials who had "misclassified" their grandparents as members of the "exploiting" class during the "class" labeling campaign in the early 1950s[5]. It never occurred to them that some people had become members of the lower caste lower class probably also because of the "misclassification".

Children's Adaptation

Lower caste middle class children gradually understood that it did not solve any problems for them to deny their lower caste origins. Adaptation to the new reality thus became an urgent task for many lower caste middle class children. This was a serious business after 1966 when it became mandatory to report one's family political status to school authorities. Lower caste middle class children knew that if their "bad class" backgrounds became known in school, they would be subject to social discrimination. They would have to do their best to conceal their "bad class" origin. To understand their actions, it is necessary to describe briefly the political dossier system in Mao's China.

Under Mao the CCP established a political dossier system as a means of control. Dossiers (*dang'an*) were files kept by the CCP on each citizen, including school children. These files usually covered an individual's complete political history. They included data on a person's family members: their ages, class background, rewards and allegiances.[6]

In addition, each dossier contained an individual's self-reports, any evaluations by peers and supervisors or teachers, and any official warnings and punishments. The dossier was retained throughout a person's life.[7] The file was consulted by superiors whenever a review was required for job application and assignment, college admission, punishment, promotion or reward of a variety of benefits.

In school, students were required to report their caste standing to teachers before registration and also to file a self-report to teachers at the end of each semester, detailing family background and political performance during the preceding half year. The teacher, upon receiving a student's self-report, would arrange for a critical assessment of it by the student's classmates. The teacher would then write an evaluation and file it in the student's dossier together with the self-report.[8]

Since the self-report card asked for the caste status of each student, it produced much anxiety among children of the lower caste middle class. It served as a reminder to their classmates of their "bad class" background. They hated filling in the self-report card, experiencing tension, shame and depression at the end of each semester when the self-report card was due.

Fortunately, lower caste middle class children found out that their teachers did not examine the accuracy of the self-report cards carefully. Teachers simply did not have the time and resources for checking each student's family class background on top of their heavy teaching and administrative duties. More importantly, the CCP never clarified, nor did the public clearly comprehend, the fine distinction between the "class" label based on family political status and that based on occupation.

Lower caste middle class children gradually understood this gray area and exploited it to their advantage. Concealing one's caste identity became a main tactic for some lower caste middle class children in dealing with the political status system. They realized that because their grandparents had been landlords or capitalists they were of "bad class" origin. Thus, if possible, they avoided mentioning their grandparents in the self-report cards. They used their parents' occupations as their family caste status. Since their parents were cadres or professionals, their family backgrounds appeared most favorable on the self-report cards.

Others excluded certain family members from the self-report cards. They listed on their report cards the names of all their relatives who were the CCP members or government officials. They did so even if their families lacked close contact with the relatives listed. Their family connections thus seemed to be extremely "revolutionary".

In addition, many lower caste middle class children maintained a low profile in school. Unlike their upper caste counterparts, they did not engage in political activism. They could not afford to do so. If politically active, their teachers might consider them candidates for leadership positions in student organizations and would investigate their families' histories thoroughly. Their "bad class" connections might then be disclosed, subjecting them to discrimination. Therefore, they removed themselves from political activism and social recognition. They remained obedient to teachers and avoided disputes with classmates. As ordinary students, not the subjects of particular attention, they were left to themselves.

Based on similar considerations, some lower caste middle class children did not apply for admission to the Communist Youth League. Were they to do so authorities would then see to it that their families' class backgrounds were reported accurately, thus possibly disclosing their "bad class" connections.

One respondent (Informant 42) told of applying for membership in the Communist Youth League when he was an educated youth in a village. Investigators from the Communist Youth League branch in his production brigade learned from his parents' work unit of his "bad class" origin. Consequently his life was made miserable. From that he learned a lesson and, upon return to his hometown for work, he avoided applying for Communist Youth League membership and was politically inactive. He experienced no discrimination and was well accepted by his co-workers who were unaware of his family background.

If the "bad class" origin of a lower caste middle class child were revealed, other coping mechanisms had to be developed to survive the political status system. One such method was political activism. Some lower caste middle class respondents migrated to the countryside after graduating from secondary school. They had chosen to live in poor villages, wanting to prove their "redness" through hard work. A few lower caste middle class children were appointed heads of their "educated youth villages".

Another coping mechanism aiding children of the lower caste middle class was aggression, that is, attacks on their fellow caste members. There were at least two advantages to this approach. First, through such attacks the child could reestablish a positive image, since this would suggest a strong desire to break away from his or her own caste.

Second, it was unwise for a lower caste person to engage in a hopeless struggle against the repressive regime and the powerful upper caste. Attacking his or her fellow lower caste members posed no danger of retaliation. As a matter of fact, if fellow lower caste members attacked him or her, it could serve as a desirable proof of his or her dissociation from the pariah group, thus creating a good chance of acceptance by people of the upper caste. Indeed, during the Cultural Revolution, some lower caste middle class children were aggressive enough to attack their parents in order to show their revolutionary consciousness. Others, however, took an easier approach by attacking other lower caste people.

One respondent (Informant 44) spoke of a "leftist" teacher in his primary school. The teacher's father was a cadre. But his grandfather was a capitalist. The respondent thought he had been more "leftist" than teachers of the working class families. He divided the students in his class into two groups according to "class" origins, ordering the children from the "bad class" families to sit on the right side of the classroom and arranging the children from the "good class" families to sit on the left side. At that time, the left stood for revolution, the right for counterrevolution. Everyday the teacher scolded the children of the lower caste and praised those from the "good class" families. The teacher proclaimed that the "good class" students were the future of China.

When political campaigns were waged, the teacher organized "good class" students in struggles against the students and teachers with "bad class" origins. Further, he continuously curried favor from the school revolutionary committee chairman. He assiduously avoided all forms of trouble throughout the Cultural Revolution. The chairman always protected him, arguing that he had broken away from the "bad class" and served as an example to the youthful members of the "exploiting class".

Family Adaptation

Unlike their lower class counterparts, lower caste middle class families were equipped with resources and adopted various devices for dealing with the political status system and for helping their children meet the challenges of the new reality. Middle class professionals possessed technical skills that were in great demand in China. They used their expertise to minimize social discrimination. One respondent (Informant 41) recounted going to a village with his parents who led peasants to accept them as medical doctors willing to provide services. The peasants were in need of their help and avoided treating them as the people of the "bad class".

Unlike lower caste lower class counterparts, lower caste middle class families were equipped with network resources to deal with social dislocation during the Cultural Revolution. A middle class respondent (Informant 21) and his brother were accused by Red Guards of engaging in "anti-revolutionary deeds". Their mother traveled to Beijing seeking help from the boys' uncle, a liaison officer of a high official in the State Council. Their uncle returned to their hometown with their mother and assisted the family.

Also unlike their lower class counterparts, families of the lower caste middle class did not accept social discrimination passively. Lower caste middle class parents had been insiders of and were thus familiar with the workings of the system in Mao's China. They often actively explored the various avenues for solutions to problems.

A middle class respondent (Informant 26) received his first self-report card while in primary school. He asked his father what family "class" status he should enter in the form. His father thought about it for a long time and told him to enter "landlord" (because his grandfather had been a landlord). From that time on he found himself under extreme pressure in school. His father learned this and wrote to the *People's Daily* asking about his son's family political status. The editor replied, stating that the father's occupation could be used as the son's family political status. Since the father was a cadre and had joined the CCP before 1949, the son became a child of the "good class". Since the *People's Daily* was the CCP's official newspaper, no one could or dared to dispute its opinion regarding his "class" designation.

Two Worlds of Childhood

The power of the political status system reached its zenith during the Cultural Revolution. The political status system was in fact a caste system, functioning as a systematic program for undermining political and economic rights of people of the "bad class", enhancing the self-esteem of people of the "good class" and promoting self-abnegating reactions from people of the "bad class".[9] Mayfair Mei-hui Yang writes that the "class"-status categories embodied different amounts of prestige, privilege, rights, virtues, and trust. To fall into one category was to be totally suffused with that particular "class" nature, to be assigned a social identity stamped by the moral-political judgments levied on that "class", and to be rewarded, avoided, or punished according to a person's "class" status. This normative technique of classification and identification infiltrated and at times inundated the conduct of the distributive economy in Mao's China.[10]

However, I have shown in this chapter that lower caste families of different socioeconomic status experienced and responded to the political status system in a variety of ways. Lower caste lower class families were persistently discriminated against. The Cultural Revolution was just another episode in a long history of suffering among these families. Conceptions of the reality that arose from life situations among these families might reduce the capacity of discrimination as a means of promoting active adaptive responses to political change.

Studies of caste societies show that orientations in the lower caste families were distinguished by feelings of timidity, by a rigid and simple conception of reality, and by a fatalistic belief that one's life was subject to the whim of ruthless external forces. Born of capricious circumstances, such orientations could only foster among these families an apathetic acceptance of humiliation.[11] I show that during the Cultural Revolution many lower caste lower class people similarly depended on habitual submission to accommodate political discrimination.

In some extreme cases, deprivation might lead to a desperate desire among lower caste lower class people to confront the upper caste people directly. However, such moves did not terminate discrimination and might worsen the situation, no matter how they ended. Lower caste lower class people confronted upper caste people not only because they felt unfairly treated, but more importantly because they were disoriented and did not know how to avoid further unfair treatments. Direct confrontation could only serve as an indicator of their inability to cope with the political status system. The lower caste lower class families were left with limited options for dealing with caste discrimination because of their low socioeconomic status. They were just not well equipped with psychological sophistication and resources to beat the political status system.

In contrast, families of the lower caste middle class enjoyed prestige and financial security before 1966. They were treated as members of the lower caste for the first time during the Cultural Revolution. Such experience turned out to be a powerful stimulus for them to redress their grievances. It is true that families of the lower caste middle class could not match the first hand experience of the lower class families in discrimination and the lessons they provided. However, middle class people tended to know more about the workings of the social system than lower class counterparts, and were more familiar with available avenues for solving problems. They were better equipped in resources and orientations to work out feasible adaptive responses to the complexities and challenges of the change.

Such differences in adaptation abilities between the middle class and the lower class are not unique to China. In his study of the Great Depression in the US, Glen H. Elder finds out that the ability to encounter deprivation was closely associated with class positions. Children from the middle class ranked higher than those from the lower class on the capacity to adapt to change and adversity. Problem-solving resources and support for adaptive responses tended to increase with class positions. Middle class children and parents also ranked higher on intellectual resources, and their conceptions of reality were more conducive to effective adaptation in situation of change and uncertainty. Deprivation has different meanings to people of different socioeconomic status.[12]

Similarly, in Mao's China, lower caste lower class children and their middle class counterparts experienced different lifestyles, displayed different values and orientations, and adopted different strategies to deal with the political status system. The life paths of the children of China's lower caste during the Cultural Revolution confirm Elder's findings once again.

Notes

1. Hong Yung Lee, *The Politics of the Cultural Revolution* (Berkeley: University of California Press, 1978); Stanley Rosen, *Red Guard Factionalism and the Cultural Revolution in Guangzhou* (Boulder: Westview Press, 1982); Jonathan Unger, "The Class System in Rural China." Pp. 121-141 in James L. Watson (ed.) *Class and Social Stratification in Post-Revolution China* (Cambridge: Cambridge University Press, 1984); Gordon White, *The Politics of Class and Class Origins* (Contemporary China Centre, The Australian National University, 1974); Lynn White, *Politics of Chaos* (Princeton: Princeton University Press, 1989).

2. Lee 1978 (footnote 1); Rosen 1982 (footnote 1); Unger 1984 (footnote 1); White 1974 (footnote 1).

3. John Dollard, *Caste and Class in a Southern Town* (New York: Doubleday, 1957); Stephen Fuchs, *Children of Hari* (Vienna: Verlag Herold, 1950).

4. Unger 1984 (footnote 1), p. 126.

5. See Chapter 2 for the class-labeling campaign in the early 1950s.

6. Andrew Walder, *Communist Neo-Traditionalism* (Berkeley: University of California Press, 1986), Pp. 91-92.

7. Walder 1986 (footnote 6).

8. Interviews.

9. Richard Kraus, *Class Conflict in Chinese Socialism* (New York: Columbia University Press, 1981); Watson 1984 (footnote 1); White 1974 (footnote 1).

10. Mayfair Mei-hui Yang, *Gifts, Favors, and Banquets* (Ithaca: Cornell University Press, 1994), p. 186.

11. E. W. Bakke, *Citizens without Work* (New Haven: Yale University Press, 1940); Glen H. Elder, *Children of the Great Depression* (Chicago: University of Chicago Press, 1974).

12. Elder 1974 (footnote 11); also see L. Thara Bhai, Changing *Patterns of Caste & Class Relations in South India* (Delhi: Gian Publishing House, 1987); Bakke 1940 (footnote 11); Allison Davis and John Dollard, *Children of Bondage* (New York: Harper Touchbooks, 1964); Dollard 1957 (footnote 3); A. K. Srivastava, *Social Class and Family Life in India* (Allahabad: Chugn Publication, 1986).

9

CLASS, CASTE AND POLITICAL BEHAVIOR IN CHINA

In the previous chapters I have studied four groups of children, focusing on the differences in their family lives, the principles that guided their participation in the Cultural Revolution, their manners of expression, and their concerns during those turbulent years. Each group operated under its own unique situation and relied on different adaptation strategies during the Cultural Revolution. The life experience of each group was different from all other three. The differences were the result of the class system and the caste hierarchy in Mao's China. Class and caste interacted with each other and influenced family life and political behavior of Chinese adolescents of different socioeconomic status.

Class and Caste in Pre-1966 China

The political status system was certainly an important dimension of social stratification in Mao's China. However, as Richard Kraus points out, "the bad classers" (the lower caste lower class people) have been invariably referred to as a stereotype of the lower caste people in Mao's China.[1] Class differentiation within the lower caste and its impact on behavior patterns have not been carefully examined.

Additionally, stratification within the upper caste (the "good class") has been understood mainly in terms of occupational groups (i.e., workers, cadres). There has not emerged a strong interest in the link between political behavior and class differentiation within these occupational groups, at least not at the empirical level.

I write this book to narrow the gap between reality and our conception of social stratification in the Mao era. I have shown that the lower caste lower class was only part of the lower caste. There was also a middle class within the lower caste. Families of lower caste middle class were different from their lower class counterparts in income, prestige, values and political orientations.

Similarly, there existed a lower class and a middle class within the upper caste, each with its own distinctive lifestyle and political orientation.

I have also shown that there were no significant distinctions between the families of the upper caste middle class and those of the lower caste middle class. Both groups enjoyed prestige and financial security. This should not come as a surprise since both groups occupied identical positions in the socioeconomic hierarchy before 1966. It is worth noting that Mao's China was not an exception. Existing studies show that stratification in income, status and privileges in caste society is determined jointly by caste and class.[2]

TABLE 9.1 Family Life and Political Behavior in the Pre-1966 Chinese Society

	The Upper Caste	*The Lower Caste*
The Middle Class	Socialization into political activism, elite students, upward mobility and high family social status, good material life	Socialization into political activism, elite students, upward mobility and high family social status, good material life
The Lower Class	Poor material life, conformity, political inactivism, ordinary students	Poor material life under constant discrimination, low family social status, poor students

Further, I have shown in previous chapters two worlds of childhood in the pre-1966 Chinese society. Unlike their lower class counterparts, middle class children of both the upper and lower castes enjoyed opportunities for upward mobility and good material life. Middle class children, regardless their caste origins, were more likely to be politically active than lower class children of both the upper and lower castes (Table 9.1). Social division was based not only on the family political status hierarchy, but also on the class system. Richard Kraus analyzes this class-caste stratification system at the conceptual level.[3] The previous chapters provide empirical support to his conceptualization.

Class, Caste, and Political Behavior during the Cultural Revolution

The political status system continued to be a very important factor in constructing perceptions and behavior during the Cultural Revolution. Children of the "good class" would take advantage of their superior caste status whenever possible. The lower caste lower class people understood their inferior caste standing and behaved humbly. Children of the lower caste middle class were less likely than children of the upper caste middle class to use political activism to claim social status. Their primary concern was security, while that of children of the upper caste middle class was social recognization. The former endeavored to conceal their caste identity while the latter sought to reestablish a positive image in public.

In addition to caste, classes were another important variable explaining political behavior during the Cultural Revolution. Socialization experience and family life varied by class, which led children of different socioeconomic status to see the world differently. They developed different aspirations and conceptions of reality. Their emotional and behavioral patterns were consistent with their family socioeconomic status.

TABLE 9.2 Political Behavior during the Cultural Revolution

	The Upper Caste	*The Lower Caste*
The Middle Class	Political activism, seeking to build up a new identity to regain lost status, desocialization	Concealing caste identity, working within the system to improve situation, low profile, political inactivism
The Lower Class	High social status, political inactivism, no desocialization experience, financial survival	Habitual submission to or desperate confrontation with the upper caste

For example, political activism was the major concern of the upper caste middle class children regardless whether or not they experienced deprivation. In comparison, children of the upper caste lower class tended to be politically inactive. Also, habitual submission to or desperate conflict with the upper caste were the dominant themes of the Cultural Revolution experience of the lower caste lower class people. In contrast, the major adaptation for the lower caste middle class people during the same period was to work within the system so as to beat the family political status system (Table 9.2).

The general picture emerging from previous chapters strongly suggests that political behavior of children of the Cultural Revolution was significantly patterned along the class lines. An adequate understanding of the class differentiation within the caste hierarchy in the pre-1966 Chinese society is essential to follow the life paths of the children of the Cultural Revolution.

Changing Patterns of Stratification in Post-Mao China

The political status system was officially abolished in 1979. Its importance to Chinese society is forever gone. The class system I have analyzed in the previous chapters has persisted into post-Mao China. The cause of class differentiation in the post-Mao era is different from that during Mao's rule.

The pre-1978 class system was primarily based on the occupational ranking system of a state socialist redistributive economy. It has played a diminishing role in class differentiation after economic reforms were instituted in 1978. One important reason is the rapid growth of a private economy since then.[4]

For example, the total number of workers employed by private entrepreneurs was only 7.5 million in 1983. It increased to 17 million in 1985,[5] 24 million in 1988,[6] and 62 million in 1997.[7] Private entrepreneurs are a big winner of the economic reforms as their income is much higher than that of workers in state or collective firms.[8]

In the early 1980s most Chinese citizens considered private entrepreneurs as ex-convicts or people who failed to gain employment in the state or collective sectors. This perception has been gradually changed. Private business people are enjoying more respect these days as China moves toward a market economy. Many people with college education have gone into private business as well.[9]

Corrupt cadres in charge of important government positions have also benefited from the post-Mao reforms. They have exploited the economic reform in many ways: (1) as privileged owners and operators of private enterprises; (2) as go-betweens and deal makers in financial transitions; (3) as preferred borrowers from local and central banks for pet projects; and (4) by illegally shifting commodities from the planned to the market sector of the economy, pocketing the price differences.[10]

In contrast, middle class intellectuals and professionals have suffered a heavy financial loss in the post-Mao era, despite the fact that they still maintain their occupational prestige. In the second half of the 1980s, even the official media began to discuss a hot issue among intellectuals and students—that professors and university graduates earned less than cab drivers and hairdressers, and that everyone earned less than private entrepreneurs.[11]

State workers have also lost their privileged position in the post-Mao era. Economic reforms have generated an equalizing trend in income distribution among urban residents working in the state and collective sectors.[12] Furthermore, the government has carried out industrial reforms demanding state enterprises to be accountable for their own losses and profits. Those that fail to compete in the market economy go out of business.[13] According to official statistics, due to the poor performance of their firms, more than three million state workers were laid off in 1998 alone. It was estimated that in the same year more than six million unemployed workers were unable to find jobs.[14]

Thus, since the 1980s, income inequality has become an increasingly important social issue. In 1985, the ratio of income difference between the highest income group and the lowest income group was 2.9: 1; in 1993, 3.8: 1. In 1996, seventy million people in China earned less than 300 yuan annually. In the same year, it was discovered that each of the one million or so private business people owned production assets worth one million Chinese yuan or more. Bank deposits in China belonging to two percent of the highest income earners totaled 1,050 billion Chinese yuan (over US$131 billions at an excange rate of US$1 = 8 Chinese yuan) in 1996.[15] It has been rumored that these accounts belong to cadres and private business people.

If this trend continues, it seems that cadres and private entrepreneurs will make up the new upper and middle class. The private economy and government offices will be two crucial factors of class differentiation. Intellectuals working in the state sector have been phased out of the privileged segment of the population as a result of their steadily deteriorating economic condition.[16] Most workers and peasants have improved their material condition but still find themselves in the lower income category.

Class and Political Behavior in Post-Mao China

The change in sources of stratification does not invalidate the basic argument presented in this book. There remain classes in China, and they are material to the study of political behavior. Class interests still pattern political behavior in the post-Mao period. The 1989 pro-democracy movement provides a good example.

First, since 1978 peasants have experienced a great improvement in their material life although many of them are still poor. They have to devote all their time and energy to work in order to take care of themselves. They are basically self-sufficient and thus did not suffer as much from the inflation in the 1980s as urban residents did. Most peasants are not interested in politics. These factors may explain why the 1989 pro-democracy movement was mainly an urban phenomenon.

A few workers participated in the 1989 pro-democracy movement because they were unhappy with cadre corruption and inflation that threatened their living standard. However, since they were able to keep their economic condition from further deterioration, workers were less displeased than intellectuals and college students. This may be one of the factors why only a few workers followed the pro-democracy movement.[17]

University students and intellectuals were the backbone of the 1989 pro-democracy crusade. Jane Macartney points out that intellectuals were unhappy with their lot, feeling theirs to be the class that had benefited least from the reforms.[18] Richard Madsen points out that their anger was compounded by a sense of injustice, seeing people they considered far less worthy than they, e.g., private entrepreneurs, making far more money. They were also bitter at the corruption among high officials. They might agree in principle with the slogan that in the reforms some people must get rich first; but many of them believed that it was the wrong groups that were getting rich.[19]

Discontent also existed among university students. Their privileged positions in society were undermined by economic reforms in the 1980s. University graduates used to be under the government job assignment system that guaranteed their employment in the state sector upon graduation. But in 1988 the government proposed to abolish the job assignment system. University graduates would be asked to search for jobs themselves, without much assistance from the state.

Further, it takes a lot of efforts and time for a person to get a university place in China. University students always consider themselves talented persons and expect a high financial return from their education. A university degree was indeed a sure way to middle class status in Mao's China. Under economic reforms this was no longer true. University students were upset by the fact that upward mobility could be achieved without a college degree. There was general unhappiness among college students as they failed to perceive a positive return on their hard academic work in the future. They saw the deterioration of intellectuals' salaries and thus their own bleak futures.

University students also voiced a host of other complaints. Their living conditions were abominable. Food served in the university dinning halls was considered inedible and dormitory lighting inadequate. Despite the terrible conditions and bleak future, college students still viewed themselves as elite in society and others as backward elements. There was a vast discrepancy between their self-perceived status and the cruel reality.

It is likely that this discrepancy led to confusion and concerns among students over their future, which in turn generated discontent and protests. Although students demanded democracy in 1989, they did not understand what democracy meant. In the first place it was not the desire for democracy that led them to the Tiananmen Square. They used slogans such as "democracy" and "freedom" in an attempt to advance their interests and improve their conditions.[20] A main goal of the student movement was to gain recognition of their status in society by party officials.[21] This can be interpreted as a desperate attempt to counter the downward mobility of intellectuals and students. It is doubtful that they would take to the streets if they were happy with their status quo and could expect a bright future.

Of course, this is not to say that intellectuals and students promoted the pro-democracy movement in 1989 only because of their downward mobility in the socioeconomic hierarchy. Other factors contributing to the 1989 democracy movement included contacts between Chinese intellectuals and Western liberal ideas during the 1980s[22] and the relatively tolerant political atmosphere under Zhao Zhiyang's regime of the 1980s. Nevertheless, a key factor that motivated students and intellectuals to go to Tiananmen Square was the erosion of their position in society.

Concluding Remarks

Robert Gamer writes that when we think of China, we "think of Mao, Red Guards waving little Red Books, water buffaloes in paddy fields, laborers wearing Dixie Cup hats, pagoda temples, the Great Wall and Forbidden City, crowds of people riding bicycles, communist officials with red stars on their caps ordering around workers in great factories, school children singing socialist songs, and a lone student stopping a tank on Tiananmen Square."[23] Michael Dutton also writes that before the 1989 Tiananmen Square Incident, the Western world relied on portraits of Chairman Mao, the Great Wall or a panda bear to understand China. After 1989, when the West thinks of China it weds it to the term "repression", utilizing it to essentialize and totalize the lives of 1.2 billion people.[24] China has been perceived as a unique society.

I agree that China is different from other countries. In particular, Mao's China represented a prototype of a state socialist country with an authoritarian tradition, coercive institutions and a unique opportunity structure. However, China is also similar to other countries in its class structure. There is an upper, middle and lower class in China as in other parts of the world. Class structure affects political behavior in China as powerfully as it does in other countries. Theories of stratification can be applied to Chinese society as productively as elsewhere.

Nevertheless, in China study, political behavior has been explained from (1) China's exotic traditional culture; or (2) communist reward systems; or (3) the caste system of the "good class" and the "bad class". We have not taken full advantage of class analysis in studying behavioral development in Chinese society.

Since the late 1980s, many scholars in the US have studied factors of social stratification in the post-Mao era.[25] The link between social class and political participation in post-Mao China has not been firmly established, however. I hope that class analysis will be used to study political behavior in the post-Mao era more frequently.

Finally, I agree that many factors influence political behavior in China. In studying political participation among Chinese people, we should not ignore the subtle way in which the political culture influences behavior, nor the role of the coercive political system on constructing political choices, nor the function of the opportunity structure on defining options.

Nevertheless, I would like to point out that none of these factors suffices for a complete study. Nor do these factors exist in isolation. They interact with the class system and one another. A complete explanation of political behavior under socialism must include how people respond to the objective conditions of their lives, and how their lives are fashioned by the socioeconomic arrangements they inherit. Everything being equal, class has a crucial impact on political behavior in China.

Notes

1. See Richard Kraus, *Class Conflict in Chinese Socialism* (New York: Columbia University Press, 1981). Kraus does not use the term "the lower caste lower class people" in his work.

2. Thara Bhai, *Changing Patterns of Caste & Class Relations in South India* (Dehli: Gian Publishing House, 1987); Stephen Fuchs, *The Children of Hari* (Vienna: Verlag Herold, 1950); K. L. Sharma, *Caste, Class, and Social Movements* (Jaipur: Rawat Publications, 1986).

3. Kraus 1981 (footnote 1).

4. Thomas Gold, "Urban Private Business and Social Change." Pp. 157-178 in Deborah Davis and Ezra Vogel (eds.) *Chinese Society on the Eve of Tiananmen* (The Council on East Asian Studies, Harvard University, 1990); Victor Nee, "A Theory of Market Transition: From Redistribution to Markets in State Socialism." *American Sociological Review* (1989) 54/5: Pp. 663-681; Victor Nee, "The Emergence of a Market Society." *American Journal of Sociology* (1995) 101/4: Pp. 908-949.

5. Chu-yuan Cheng, *Behind the Tiananmen Massacre* (Boulder: Westview Press, 1990), p. 16.

6. Cheng 1990 (footnote 5), p. 16; Gold 1990 (footnote 4).

7. State Statistical Bureau, *China Statistical Yearbook 1998* (Beijing: China Statistical Publishing House, 1998), p. 131.

8. Gold 1990 (footnote 4); Margaret M. Pearson, *China's New Business Elite* (Berkeley: University of California Press, 1997); David L. Wank, *Commodifying Communism* (Cambridge: Cambridge University Press, 1999).

9. Gold 1990 (footnote 4); Pearson1997 (footnote 8); Wank 1999 (footnote 8).

10. Maria Chang, "The Meaning of the Tiananmen Incident." *Global Affairs* (Fall 1989), Pp. 12-35; Wank 1999 (footnote 8).

11. Jane Macartney, "The Students: Hero, Pawns, or Power-Brokers?" Pp. 3-23 in George Hicks (ed.) *The Broken Mirror* (Chicago: St. James Press, 1990).

12. Andrew Walder, "Economic Reform and Income Distribution in Tianjin, 1976-1986." Pp. 135-156 in Davis and Vogel 1990 (footnote 4).

13. Xiaowei Zang, "Industrial Management Systems and Managerial Ideologies in China." *Journal of Northeast Asian Studies* (Spring 1995) 14/1: Pp 80-104.

14. Yang Yiyong, "*Dangqian Zhongguo Jiuye Xingshi Fenxi.*" (An Analysis of the Labor Market in China.), *Zhongguo Qingnian*, no. 8 (1999): Pp 9-10.

15. Yang Jisheng, "*Touguo Cunzhe Kan Zhonggu.*" (Relying on Saving Accounts to Understand China.), *Zhongguo Qingnian*, no. 10 (1996): Pp. 60-62.

16. It is likely that professionals will become part of the middle class again once a market society is fully developed in China. Human capital then will function again as an important stratifying element.

17. Workers did not experience significant wage reduction or unemployment at that time, see Walder 1990 (footnote 12).

18. Macartney 1990 (footnote 11).

19. Richard Madsen, "The Spiritual Crisis of China's Intellectuals." Pp. 243-260 in Davis and Vogel 1990 (footnote 4).

20. Chalmers Johnson, "Forward." Pp. vii-xiv in Hicks 1990 (footnote 11); Macartney 1990 (footnote 11); Lucian Pye, "Tiananmen and Chinese Political Culture: The Escalation of Confrontation." Pp. 162-179 in Hicks 1990 (footnote 11).

21. Hick 1990 (footnote 11); Jeffery Wasserstrom and Elizabeth Perry (eds.) *Popular Protest and Political Culture in Modern China* (Boulder: Westview, 1992).

22. Madsen 1990 (footnote 19); Stanley Rosen, "The Impact of Reform Policies on Youth Attitudes." Pp. 283-305 in Davis and Vogel 1990 (footnote 4); Wasserstrom and Perry 1992 (footnote 21).

23. Robert E. Gamer, *Understanding Contemporary China* (Boulder: Lynn Rienner, 1999), p. 1.

24. Michael Dutton, *Streetlife China* (Cambridge: Cambridge University Press, 1998), p. 17.

25. Yanjie Bian, *Work and Inequality in Urban China* (Albany: State University of New York Press, 1994); Yanjie Bian, "Bringing Strong Ties Back In." *American Sociological Review* (1997), 62/3: Pp. 366-385; Yanjie Bian and John Logan, "Market Transition and Income Inequality in Urban China." *American Sociological Review* (1996) 61/5: Pp. 739-758; Barbara Entwisle, Gail E. Henderson, Susan E. Short, Jill Bouma, and Zhai Fengying, "Gender and Family Businesses in Rural China." *American Sociological Review* (1995) 60/1: Pp.36-57; Nee 1989 (footnote 4); Nee 1995 (footnote 4); Andrew Walder, "Property Rights and Stratification in Socialist Redistributive Economies." *American Sociological Review* (1992), 57/4: Pp. 524-539; Andrew Walder, "Career Mobility and the Communist Political Order." *American Sociological Review* (1995), 60/3: Pp. 309-328; Xie Yu and Emily Hannum, "Regional Variation in Earning Inequality in Reform-Era Urban China." *American Journal of Sociology* (1996) 101/4: Pp.950-992; Xueguang Zhou, Nancy Brandon Tuma, and Phyllis Moen, "Institutional Change and Job-Shift Patterns in Urban China, 1949 to 1994." *American Sociological Review* (1997), 62/3: Pp. 393-365.

Appendix
Notes on Methodology

Interviews

This book is based in large part on three sources of information: (1) Chinese newspaper accounts, official documents and statistics; (2) scholarly books and articles published by Chinese and Western scholars; (3) in-depth interviews with fifty-seven Chinese adults residing in the San Francisco Bay Area in 1990-1991. The last source was the most important one as it forced me to reformulate my research questions and shaped the way I interpreted family life and political behavior in Mao's China.

During the course of field interviews, I found many people cooperative. In the early stage of my fieldwork, I arranged a few interviews by telephone appointments. I discovered later that drop-by visits to the homes of potential interviewees were less formalistic but equally welcomed. Such visits may be considered highly inappropriate by Western standards but not by Chinese ones. It is in fact a cultural practice. Chinese people are used to drop-in visits and my informants were quite familiar with the custom. In China, it was hard at the time to have access to telephones. A telephone-scheduled appointment was unrealistic and looked unnatural in the eyes of Chinese. I came to realize this after the first five or six interviews. Subsequently I just dropped by the respondents' homes for interviews at a time considered convenient to them and was welcome in most cases. I was glad to realize that data collection methods would not be effective without taking the cultural context into consideration.

At the beginning of each interview I spent a great deal of time making sure that the respondent understood the purpose and design of my research. This was aimed at helping him or her to understand that my work was all about the Cultural Revolution. Since the Chinese government has officially criticised the Cultural Revolution, a discussion of the subject bears no political risk. I also guaranteed anonymity to the interviewee.

The interviews were based on a format of self-narrative life history. I asked each interviewee to recollect his or her personal experience in Mao's China. I also asked them to recall information about classmates and teachers so that I could collect as much information on the Mao era as possible.

The interviews were open-ended to allow me to clarify certain issues and probe possible answers. After the interview I returned home and took notes. I did not use a tape-recorder or notebook in the interviews so as to avoid any discomfort the respondent might have.

Although my interviews were conducted loosely, they were not devoid of structure. I repeated the same lines of questioning to each respondent with a focus on three levels of events: (1) family life; (2) early socialization experience and political attitudes; and (3) behavioral patterns before and during the Cultural Revolution.

The basic assumption behind my interview design was that family life should have a big impact on the respondent's early socialization. It in turn should influence directly or indirectly on his or her political attitudes and behavior. The Cultural Revolution should have a feedback influence on an adolescent's political attitudes and patterns of participation in politics.

Critics of the interview method usually question the reliability of interview materials. Two problems about informant reliability are salient. First, how do we know informants relate true stories? There is no guarantee that my interview materials accurately reflect the interviewees' experience in the Cultural Revolution. I do consider their stories reliable overall.

First, most of the interviewees were my family friends, acquaintances or neighbors. They were willing to be interviewed only because they wanted to help me finish my project; they were not induced or coerced in any way to answer my questions. Being a graduate student, I was unable to offer any financial rewards for their participation. And I told them I would understand if they did not wish to participate. Eleven people whom I barely knew or not at all declined to be interviewed.

Second, my interviewees were hard-working students or workers. They had better things to do with their time than making up stories for me. And it was hard for me to imagine that their detailed recollections were fabricated since my drop-in visits were of short notice, allowing little if any time to prepare fictional accounts.

The second concern regarding informant reliability is just how accurate is the recorded testimony. This is a difficult problem. As John L. Saari points out, a child, being accessible only indirectly through memory, is in fact a creation of an adult interviewer and an adult interviewee, both of whom aspire to bring the child back to the present. The narrator would recover the child within the boundaries of his or her memory. The interviewer should be aware, or made aware, of how selective and mythmaking the remembering ego can be.[1]

For example, in the interview process, sore points may be skirted consciously and later adult identities may distort the characterization of childhood. Self-reporting seems to run the risk that respondents would present to the interviewer what is deemed to be desirable rather than accurate pictures.

However, questions over informant reliability shall not deter scientific exploration. Before the 1980s, Western scholars seldom had the opportunity to do fieldwork in China. This did not prevent them from using émigré interviews to advance our overall understanding of Chinese society.

Of course a researcher needs to treat émigré testimony carefully. Andrew Walder advises that a method of "triangulation" can be used to ensure the reliability of émigré interviews, that is, a researcher shall interview as many émigrés as possible about the same event or institution and check with his or her observation. The researcher shall push informants for as much detail and clarity as possible, constantly compare the accounts of different informants, and cover the familiar ground endlessly. This cross-examination will facilitate the researcher to reach a well-grounded conclusion.[2]

I followed these techniques to deal with informant reliability. In addition, I focused on specific questions and asked respondents to provide further information to support their answers. If I asked a respondent to name a role model in his or her childhood about whom I had a fair amount of knowledge, I also asked him or her to describe the role model briefly. Because interviews were focused upon informants' personal lives, their recollections were full of detailed stories. For example, the "enemies" that were subject to personality character assassinations by some informants were either their rival classmates, manipulative teachers, unfriendly neighbors or their parents' colleagues guilty of attacking their families during the Cultural Revolution.

Furthermore, as Andrew Walder points out, a researcher working with émigrés may not have a number of informants from a single setting, but a number of informants from a single type of setting. One cannot use the method of "triangulation" commonly practiced in fieldwork if people are not talking about the same institution and the same events. But one can still compare reports about similar types of settings on the same topics and perform triangulation at a somewhat higher level of generality—less reliable for specific events, but not less reliable for general structures and social behaviors. In fact, this last point is an advantage: since the informants are drawn from a large number of similar settings, the findings are more readily generalizable than those obtained in conventional field ethnography.[3]

During the interviews, I was surprised to find out that many events that occurred in my hometown also took place in a similar fashion in many other towns or cities far, far away. I did not find significant inconsistencies between my memory of Mao's China and those of my interviewees. I also noticed that informants of the same class background, regardless of differences in birthplace, academic major, age and gender, often provided similar information of many important events and institutions.

Of course this is not to imply that each of the informants did not have his or her own biases. Nor were their recollections one hundred percent accurate. The incidents and political attitudes they recalled were not entirely fresh in their memories. But I believe that my informants tried to answer my questions as precisely and honestly as they could. My knowledge about family life and political behavior in Mao's China has greatly strengthened my confidence in the general pattern of social life and political behavior as described in the interviews.

For more information about my informants and their demographic data, their parents' education and occupations, please see Appendixes A, B, and C of my 1992 dissertation submitted to the University of California at Berkeley.

Interview Procedures

As most field researchers do, I followed new leads in the interviews, which allowed me to develop a detailed understanding of the class structure and the caste system. At the same time, my interview format ensured that I collected qualitatively comparative data on each respondent. I developed and refined my theoretical perspective and interview methods at every stage in the research process.

I have found it amazing that most researchers experience a similar situation in doing fieldwork. As Kathleen Garson points out, at the early stage of the interview process, "surprises" and interesting information kept emerging. At the late stage the researcher had accumulated a great deal of useful information and was able to predict the basic results of the next interview. In her words, "saturation" was achieved, and additional interviews seemed to be only marginally useful.[4] This was exactly what happened to me during my fieldwork.

In the presentation of quoted material in this book, occasional quotes were edited slightly for clarity. This editorial decision was also designed to eliminate traces that might reveal a respondent's identity. All respondent names were removed to assure anonymity. To facilitate the flow of the argument, one or two quotes were typically chosen to support a point, even though many examples were available.

Sample Representativeness

One major goal of this book is to describe and analyze adolescent political behavior and the emotional structure that ran parallel to the class structure in Mao's China. Such a study requires (1) a detailed description of the daily life of families of different classes; (2) the extent the Cultural Revolution affected family members economically, socially and psychologically; and (3) reaction patterns of family members to the stress that prevailed during the Cultural Revolution.

Unfortunately, there has been no systematic recording of family history in Mao's China, official or unofficial. Nor is statistics on the Cultural Revolution available. At the time of my dissertation research (1990-1991) it was impossible for me to go to China and draw a large and representative sample of veterans of the Cultural Revolution.[5] Doing field research in China required a local sponsor and financial resources, both of which were out of my reach. I had to base my research project on interviews with Chinese immigrants in the San Francisco Bay Areas. At that time, most published works on contemporary

Chinese society relied on émigré testimony. Émigré interviews were the next best thing to systematic sampling.

Picking up informants in Hong Kong was another option. But it was a financially impossible task for me. Nevertheless, I was able to justify my San Francisco Bay Area interviews by thinking that there was no guarantee that the "quality" of the Hong Kong émigrés would be any better than that of the U.S. émigrés.

I further justified my San Francisco Bay Area interviews by thinking that as a "foreigner" in Hong Kong, I did not have local contacts. I believed that I would have had a hard time locating informants and insuring informant reliability. In contrast, I had a great deal of background knowledge about my informants in the San Francisco Bay Area since I had known most of them for some time.

There is another problem with this study. The sample contained only fifty-seven respondents and thus was small. It was also unfortunately not a representative sample. Émigrés are a highly self-selected group in terms of age, sex, education, and other attributes. I was not successful in securing comradely support for my research from other scholars working on émigré interviews. To my disappointment there has been little discussion of sample representativeness in their works.

It is not clear why many scholars have discussed informant reliability at length but have overlooked sample representativeness, a crucial factor in constructing validity. My anxiety over validity was gradually reduced after I had realized that it was untrue that a scientific work had to be based on a representative sample. Were it otherwise anthropology and history should be eliminated since they do not rely on large-scale randomly selected samples.

In fact, sample representativeness is a relatively recent concept. It did not exist when Karl Marx and Max Weber wrote their sociological works. There is no doubt though that their works are masterpieces of sociology. Many good sociological studies are not based on representative samples. A few examples are *Street Corner Society* by William Foote Whyte,[6] *Tally's Corner* by Elliot Liebow,[7] *Caste and Class in a Southern Town* by John Dollard,[8] and *Honor and the American Dream* by Ruth Horowitz.[9]

I understand that the power of their works does not lie in the quality of their samples. A biased sample does not always lead to a biased conclusion. A researcher depends on his or her sample for evidence, but he or she is also equipped with theoretical guidance and conceptual tools to make scientific analysis. A good theory and a good analytical ability are very important when a researcher lacks a representative sample.

Of course it is not true that theory is extremely powerful and that all studies based on unrepresentative samples can depend on good theories to yield sound findings. A researcher is likely to make mistakes if he or she is interested in inducing a new theory from an unrepresentative sample.

My study, however, is somewhat immunized from such dangers; it was not designed for a grandiose discovery. Rather, I aimed to validate a well-founded theory. That is, there is a class system in any society that influences family life and adolescent political behavior. As a matter of fact, there would be a great deal of doubt about the sample and the findings of my study had it refuted this theory.

I have learned from Kathleen Garson's work that it is not true that a large and representative sample is not desirable for a sociological inquiry. Everything else being equal, a large and randomly selected sample is always preferable to an unrepresentative and small one in terms of statistical reliability and representativeness.[10] However, in the case of this study, the benefits of collecting qualitative, in-depth information outweighed sacrifices in sample size and sample representativeness.

Kathleen Ganson also points out that there is no doubt that ideas discovered by this kind of qualitative research await systematic verification on large random samples. But without this stage of small-scale, exploratory research, the findings presented here might not have been uncovered.[11]

Finally, the aim of my study is not to predict the exact percentage of Chinese that would behave in one way or the other, but to uncover the social forces that led children of different class backgrounds to choose whatever paths they took in Mao's China. The ideas developed in this book can then be tested and refined with a large representative sample that allows comparisons among other groups of Chinese of other age cohorts and of other social status. I hope that this book will be a part of exploratory work of social research out of which more authoritative descriptions of reality in China will emerge.

Other Sources

I also collected information from official documents (such as *Red Flag* and *People's Daily*) and from unofficial data sources such as Red Guard publications. In addition, I read some recollections of the Cultural Revolution by former Red Guards and went through some reportage on the Cultural Revolution. I cross-examined data in the official press with those in "unofficial" (the Red Guard) press and with data in Western publications. The material gathered from these sources played a secondary role in this study. They helped me refresh my memories of the Cultural Revolution and provided some background information.

Notes

1. John Saari, *Legacies of Childhood* (San Francisco: Jossey-Bass Publishers, 1977).

2. Andrew Walder, "The Hong Kong Interviews: An Essay on Method." Pp. 255-269 in Andrew Walder, *Communist Neo-Traditionalism* (Berkeley: University of California Press, 1986).

3. Walder 1986 (footnote 2).

4. Kathleen Garson, "Methodology." Pp. 240-247 in Kathleen Garson, *Hard Choices* (Berkeley: University of California Press, 1985).

5. Western scholars have been able to conduct large-scale surveys to study the Cultural Revolution in the late 1990s. See Xueguang Zhou and Liren Hou, "Children of the Cultural Revolution: The State and the Life Course in the People's Republic of China." *American Sociological Review* (1999) 64/1: Pp. 12-36.

6. William Foote Whyte, *Street Corner Society (Chicago: University of Chicago Press, 1955).*

7. Elliot Liebow, *Tally's Corner* (Boston: Little, Brown, 1967).

8. John Dollard *Caste and Class in a Southern Town* (New York: Doubdleday Anchor Books, 1957).

9. Ruth Horowitz *Honor and the American Dream* (New Bruswick: Rutgers University Press, 1986).

10. Garson 1985 (footnote 4).

11. Garson 1985 (footnote 4).

Bibliography

Bakke, Wight E. 1940. *Citizens without Work.* New Haven: Yale University Press.

Balasz, Etienne. 1974. *Chinese Civilization and Bureaucracy.* New Haven: Yale University Press.

Barnett, A. Doak and Ralph N. Clough. (eds.) 1986. *Modernizing China.* Boulder: Westview Press.

Barker, Randolph and Radha Sinha. (eds.) 1982. *The Chinese Agricultural Economy.* Boulder: Westview Press.

Barnouin, Barbara and Yu Changgen (eds.) 1993. *Ten Years of Turbulence.* London and New York: Kegan Paul International.

Bendix, Reinhard and Seymour Martin Lipset. (eds.) 1953. *Class, Statues and Power.* Glencoe: The Free Press.

Bergere, Marie-Claire. 1989. *The Golden Age of the Chinese Bourgeoisie, 1911-1937.* Cambridge: Cambridge University Press.

Bhai, L. Thara. 1987. *Changing Patterns of Caste & Class Relations in South India.* Delhi: Gian Publishing House.

Bian, Yanjie. 1994. *Work and Inequality in Urban China.* Albany: State University of New York Press.

Yanjie Bian. 1997. "Bringing Strong Ties Back In." *American Sociological Review* 62/3: Pp. 366-385

Bian, Yanjie and John Logan. 1996. "Market Transition and Income Inequality in Urban China." *American Sociological Review* 61/5: Pp. 739-758.

Billeter, Jean-Francois. 1985. "The System of 'Class Status.'" Pp. 127-169 in *The Scope of State Power in China* (ed.) Stuart R. Scharm. London: School of Oriental and African Studies, University of London.

Bronfenbrenner, Urie. 1958. "Socialization and Social Class through Space and Time." Pp. 400-425 in *Readings in Social Psychology* (eds.) Eleanor E. Maccoby, Theodore Newcomber, and Engene L. Hartley. New York: Henry Holt and Co.

Burns, John. 1988. *Political Participation in Rural China.* Berkeley: University of California Press.

Cao, Zhi. 1985. *Zhonghua Renmin Gongheguo Renshizhidu Gangyao* (An Outline of Personnel Policies of the PRC). Beijing: Beijing University Press.

Chan, Anita. 1985. *Children of Mao.* Seattle: University of Washington Press.

Chan, Anita, Richard Madsen, and Jonathan Unger. 1980. "Students and Class Warfare: the Social Roots of the Red Guard Conflict in Guangzhou (Canton)." *The China Quarterly* (September) no. 83: Pp. 397-446.

Chan, Anita, Richard Madsen, and Jonathan Unger. 1984. *Chan Village.* Berkeley: University of California Press.

Chang, Chung-li. 1955. *The Chinese Gentry.* Seattle: University of Washington Press.

Chang, Maria. 1989. "The Meaning of the Tiananmen Incident." *Global Affairs* (Fall): Pp. 12-35.

Chang, Parris H. 1975. *Power and Policy in China.* University Park: The Pennsylvania State University Press.

Chen, Ruoxi. 1982. *Democracy Wall and the Unofficial Journals.* Center for Chinese Studies, University of California, Berkeley.

Chen, Zhili. 1991. *Zhongguo Gongchandang Jiandangshi* (A History of the Chinese Communist Party). Shanghai: People's Press.

Cheng, Chu-yuan. 1990. *Behind the Tiananmen Massacre.* Boulder: Westview Press.

Cheng, Tiejun and Mark Selden. 1994. "The Origins and Social Consequences of China's Hukou System." *The China Quarterly* (September) no. 139: Pp. 644-668

Christensen, Harold. (ed.) 1964. *The Handbook of Marriage and the Family.* Chicago: Rand McNally.

Ch'u, T'ung-tsu. 1957. "Chinese Class Structure and Its Ideology," Pp. 235-250 in *Chinese Thought and Institutions* (ed.) John K. Fairbank. Chicago: University of Chicago Press.

Clapham, Christopher. (ed.) 1982. *Private Patronage and Public Power, Political Clientelism in the Modern State.* London: Frances Pinter.

Connor, Walter. 1979. *Socialism, Politics, and Equality.* New York: Columbia University Press.

Coopersmith, Stanley. 1967. *The Antecedents of Self-Esteem.* San Francisco: W. H. Freeman and Company.

Croll, Elizabeth. 1981. *The Politics of Marriage in Contemporary China.* Cambridge: Cambridge University Press.

Davis, Allison and John Dollard. 1964. *Children of Bondage.* New York: Harper Touchbooks.

Davis, Deborah and Ezra Vogel. (eds.) 1990. *Chinese Society on the Eve of Tiananmen.* Cambridge: The Council on East Asian Studies, Harvard University.

Dawley, Alan. 1979. *Class and Community.* Cambridge: Harvard University Press.

Deng, Xian. 1993. *Zhongguo Zhiqing Meng* (The Dream of the Educated Youth in China). Beijing: Renmin Wenxue Chubanshe.

Donnithorne, Audrey. 1967. *China's Economic System.* London: George Allen and Unwin.

Denzin, Norman. 1977. *Childhood Socialization.* San Francisco: Jossey-Bass Publishers.

Dittmer, Lowell. 1974. *Liu Shao-chi and the Chinese Cultural Revolution.* Berkeley: University of California Press.

Dollard, John. 1949 (1957). *Caste and Class in a Southern Town.* New York: Doubleday, Anchor Books.

Dutton, Michael. 1998. *Streetlife China.* Cambridge: Cambridge University Press.

Eisenstadt, Shmuel Noah and Gene Lemarchand. (eds.) 1981. *Political Clientelism, Patronage and Development.* Berveley Hill: Sage Publications.

Elder, Glen H. 1965. "Role Relations, Socio-Cultural Environment and Autocratic Family Ideology." *Sociometry* (June) 28: Pp. 173-96.

Elder, Glen H. 1974. *Children of the Great Depression.* Chicago: University of Chicago Press.

Elder, Glen H. 1985. "Perspectives on the Life Course." Pp. 23-49 in *Life Course Dynamics: Trajectories and Transitions, 1968-1980* (ed.) Glen H. Elder. Ithaca: Cornell University Press.

Elder, Glen H. (ed.) 1985. *Life Course Dynamics: Trajectories and Transitions, 1968-1980.* Ithaca: Cornell University Press.

Elder, Glen H. 1995. "The Life Course Paradigm: Social Change and Individual Development." Pp. 101-139 in *Examining Lives in Context* (eds.) Phyllis Moen, Glen H. Elder, and Kurt Luscher. Wastington DC: American Psychological Association.

Elvin, Mark. 1973. *The Pattern of the Chinese Past.* Stanford: Stanford University Press.

Emerson, John. 1971. "Manpower Training and Utilization of Specialized Cadres, 1949-1968." Pp. 183-214 in *The City in Communist China* (ed.) John Lewis. Stanford: Stanford University Press.

Entwisle, Barbara, Gail E. Henderson, Susan E. Short, Jill Bouma, and Zhai Fengying. 1995. "Gender and Family Businesses in Rural China." *American Sociological Review* 60/1: Pp. 36-57.

Faber, Bernard Lewis. (ed.) 1976. *The Social Structure of East Europe.* New York: Praeger.

Fairbank, John K. (ed.) 1957. *Chinese Thought and Institutions.* Chicago: University of Chicago Press.

Fairbank, John K. 1969. *Trade and Diplomacy on the China Coast.* Cambridge: Harvard University Press.

Falkenheim, Victor. (ed.) 1989. *Chinese Politics from Mao to Deng.* New York: Paragon House.

Fei, Hsiao-tung. 1980. *China's Gentry.* Chicago: The University of Chicago Press.

Field, Robert Michael. 1983. "Slow Growth of Labor Productivity in Chinese Industry, 1951-1981." *The China Quarterly* (December) no. 96: Pp. 647-650.

Frolic, Michael. 1980. *Mao's People.* Cambridge: Harvard University Press.

Fuchs, Stephen. 1950. *Children of Hari.* Vienna: Verlag Herold.

Gamer, Robert E. 1999. *Understanding Contemporary China.* Boulder: Lynn Rienner.

Gardner, John. 1971. "Educated Youth and Urban-Rural Inequalities, 1958-1966." Pp. 235-286 in *The City in Communist China* (ed.) John Lewis. Stanford: Stanford University Press.

Garson, Kathleen. 1985. *Hard Choices.* Berkeley: University of California Press.

George, Linda K. 1993. "Sociological Perspective on Life Transitions." *Annual Review of Sociology* 19: Pp. 353-373.

Gerth, Hans H. and C. W. Mills. (eds.) 1958. *From Marx Weber.* New York: Oxford University Press.

Goffman, Erving. 1959. *The Presentation of Self.* New York: Doubleday.

Gold, Thomas. 1990. "Urban Private Business and Social Change." Pp. 157-178 in *Chinese Society on the Eve of Tiananmen* (eds.) Deborah Davis and Ezra Vogel. Cambridge: The Council on East Asian Studies, Harvard University.

Gold, Thomas. 1991. "State and Youth." *The China Quarterly* (December) no. 127: Pp. 594-612.

Gouldner, Alvin and William Peterson. 1961. *Notes on Technology and the Moral Order.* Indianapolis: Bobbs-Merrill.

Grey, Alan. 1969. *Class and Personality.* New York: Atherton Press.

Hansen, Donald and Reuben Hill. 1964. "Families under Stress." Pp. 695-723 in *The Handbook of Marriage and the Family* (ed.) Harold Christensen. Chicago: Rand McNally.

Hao, Yen-p'ing. 1986. *The Commercial Revolution in Nineteenth-Century China.* Berkeley: University of California Press.

Harding, Harry. 1981. *Organizing China.* Stanford: Stanford University Press.

Harding, Harry. 1989. *China's Second Revolution.* Washington DC: The Brooking Institute.

Harrison, James Pinckney. 1972. *The Long March to Power: A History of the Chinese Communist Party, 1921-1972.* New York: Praeger.

Hauser, Robert. 1971. *Socioeconomic Background and Educational Performance.* The Arnold and Caroline Rose Monograph Series in Sociology, American Sociology Association.

Heng, Liang and Judith Shapiro. 1983. *Son of the Revolution.* New York: Vintage.

Hicks, George. 1990. (ed.) *The Broken Mirror.* Chicago: St. James Press.

Hinton, William. 1966. *Fanshen.* New York: Vintage Books.

Ho, Ping-Ti. 1962. *The Ladder of Success in Imperial China.* New York: Columbia University Press.

Hollingshead, August B. 1949. *Elmtown's Youth.* New York: John Wiley & Sons.

Horowitz, Ruth. 1986. *Honor and the American Dream.* New Bruswick: Rutgers University Press.

Houn, Franklin. 1957. "The Eighth Central Committee of the Chinese Communist Party." *American Political Science Review* 51/2: Pp. 392-404.

Huang, Philip CC. 1990. *The Peasant Family and Rural Development in the Yangzi Delta, 1350-1988.* Stanford: Stanford University Press.

Huang, Shaorong. 1996. *To Rebel Is Justified: A Rhetorical Study of China's Cultural Revolution Movement 1966-1969.* Lanham: University Press of America.

Inkeles, Alex. 1950. "Social Stratification and Mobility in the Soviet Union." *American Sociological Review* 15: Pp. 465-479.

Inkeles, Alex and Peter Rossi. 1956. "National Comparisons of Occupational Prestige." *American Journal of Sociology* 61: Pp. 329-339.

Inkeles, Alex and Raymond Bauer. 1961. *The Soviet Citizen.* Cambridge: Harvard University Press.

Israel, John. 1966. *Student Nationalism in China, 1927-1937.* Stanford: Hoover Institution Publications.

Johnson, Chalmers. (ed.) 1970. *Change in Communist Systems.* Stanford: Stanford University Press.

Johnson, Chalmers. 1990. "Foreword." Pp. vii-xiv in *The Broken Mirror* (ed.) George Hicks. Chicago: St. James Press.

Joseph, William A., Christine Wong, and David Zweig (eds.) 1991. *New Perspectives on the Cultural Revolution.* Cambridge: Council on East Asian Studies, Harvard University.

Klein, Donald W. and Lois B. Hager. 1971. "The Ninth Central Committee." *The Chinese Quarterly* (January/March) no. 45: Pp. 37-56.

Klein, Donald and John Israel. 1976. *Rebels and Bureaucrats: China's December 9ers.* Berkeley: University of California Press.

Kohn, Melvin. 1977. *Class and Conformity.* Chicago: University of Chicago Press.

Kraus, Richard. 1981. *Class Conflict in Chinese Socialism.* New York: Columbia University Press.

Kraus, Richard. 1989. *Pianos & Politics in China.* New York: Oxford University Press.

Krauss, Irving. 1976. *Stratification, Class, and Conflict.* New York: The Free Press.

Kwong, Julia. 1988. *The Cultural Revolution in China's School.* Stanford: Hoover Institution Press.

Kuhn, Philip A. 1984. "Chinese Views of Social Classification." Pp. 16-28 in *Class and Social Stratification in Post-Revolution China* (ed.) James L. Watson. Cambridge: Cambridge University Press.

Lang , Olga. 1946. *Chinese Family and Society.* New Haven: Yale University Press.

Lardy, Nicolas. 1983. *Agriculture in China's Modern Economic Development.* Cambridge: Cambridge University Press.

Lasswell, Thomas. 1965. *Class and Stratum.* Boston: Houghton Mifflin Company.

Lee, Hong Yung. 1978. *The Politics of the Cultural Revolution.* Berkeley: University of California Press.

Lee, Hong Yung. 1991. *From Revolutionary Cadres to Party Technocrats in Socialist China.* Berkeley: University of California Press.

Lewis, John. (ed.) 1971. *The City in Communist China.* Stanford: Stanford University Press.

Li, Guoying. 1985. *Shehui Zhuyi Gongzi Gailan* (An Outline of the Socialist Wage System). Changchun: Jinlin Renmin Chubanshe.

Li, Weiyi. 1991. *Zhongguo Gongzi Zhidu* (Wage Systems in China). Beijing: Zhongguo Laodong Chubanshe.

Li, Zhu. 1991. "*Shixi Woguo Naotishouru Bizhong de Shiheng* (An Analysis of Causes for Unfair Distribution of Income between Mental and Manual Workers in Our Country)." *Lanzhou Xuekan*, no. 2: Pp. 65-70.

Library Section, The Institute of Philosophy, China Social Sciences Academy. 1980. *Sanshinian Jieji he Jiejidouzheng Lunwen Xuanji* (Selected Works on Class and Class Struggle for the Past 30 Years). Beijing: China Social Sciences Academy.

Liebow, Elliot. 1967. *Tally's Corner*. Boston: Little & Brown.

Lin, Jing. 1991. *The Red Guards' Path to Violence: Political, Educational, and Psychological Factors*. New York: Praeger.

Lin, Nan and Wen Xie. 1988. "Occupational Prestige in Urban China." *American Journal of Sociology* 93 /4: Pp. 793-832.

Linbeck, John. (ed.) *China: Management of A Revolutionary Society*. Seattle: University of Washington Press.

Lipman, Jonathan and Steven Harrell. (eds.) *Violence in China*. Albany: State University of New York Press

Liu, Alan 1976. *Political Culture and Group Conflict in Communist China*. Santa Barbara: Clio Books.

Lo, Fulang. 1989. *Morning Breeze*. San Francisco: China Books & Periodicals.

Lowenthall, Richard. 1970. "Development vs. Utopia in Communist Policy." Pp. 33-116 in *Change in Communist Systems* (ed.) Chalmers Johnson. Stanford: Stanford University Press.

Lu, Xinhua et al. (Gerenie Barme and Bennet Lee, trans.) 1979. *The Wounded*. Hong Kong: Joing Publishing Company.

Macartney, Jane. 1990. "The Students: Hero, Pawns, or Power-Brokers?" Pp. 3-23 in *The Broken Mirror* (ed.) George Hicks. Chicago: St. James Press.

Maccoby, Eleanor E, Theodore Newcomber, and Engene L. Hartley. (eds.) 1958. *Readings in Social Psychology*. New York: Henry Holt and Co.

MacFarquhar, Roderick. 1974. *Origins of the Cultural Revolution Vol. I*. New York: Columbia University Press.

Madsen, Richard. 1990. "The Politics of Revenge in Rural China during the Cultural Revolution." Pp. 175-202 in *Violence in China* (eds.) Jonathan Lipman and Steven Harrell. Albany: State University of New York Press.

Madsen, Richard. 1990. "The Spiritual Crisis of China's Intellectuals." Pp. 243-260 in *Chinese Society on the Eve of Tiananmen* (eds.) Deborah Davis and Ezra Vogel. Cambridge: The Council on East Asian Studies, Harvard University.

Mallee, Hein. 1995. "China's Household Registration System under Reform." *Development and Change* 26/1: Pp. 1-29

Mao, Zedong. 1969. "An Analysis of the Classes in Chinese Society." Pp. 3-11 in *Mao Zedong Xanji* (Selected Works of Mao Zedong). (ed.) Zhonggong Zhongyang Mao Zedong Xuanji Chuban Weiyuanhui. Beijing: People's Press.

Marthews, Mervyn. 1989. "Residence Controls in Present-Day China." *Asian Affairs* 20/2: Pp. 184-194

May, Ernest R. and John K. Fairbank (eds.) 1986. *America's China Trade in Historical Perspective*. The Council on East Asian Studies, Harvard University.

McKinley, Donald. 1963. *Social Class and Family Life*. Glencoe: The Free Press.

Mills, C. Wright. 1959. *The Sociological Imagination*. New York: Oxford University Press.

Moen, Phyllis, Glen H. Elder, and Kurt Luscher. (eds.) 1995. *Examining Lives in Context*. Wastington DC: American Psychological Association.

Mu, Fu-sheng. 1963. *The Wilting of the Hundred Flowers: the Chinese Intelligentsia under Mao*. New York: Praeger.

Munro, Donald. 1971. "Egalitarian Ideal and Educational Fact in Communist China." Pp. 256-301 in *China: Management of A Revolutionary Society* (ed.) John Linbeck. Seattle: University of Washington Press.

Nathan, Andrew. 1986. *Chinese Democracy*. Berkeley: University of California Press.

Nee, Victor. 1989. "A Theory of Market Transition: From Redistribution to Markets in State Socialism." *American Sociological Review* 54/5: Pp. 663-681.

Nee, Victor. 1995. "The Emergence of a Market Society." *American Journal of Sociology* 101/4: Pp. 908-949.

North, Robert and Ithiel Pool. 1952. *Kuomintang and Chinese Communist Elites*. Stanford: Stanford University Press.

Oi, Jean. 1985. "Communism and Clientelism." *World Politics* 3/2: Pp. 328-366.

Parish, L. William. 1984. "Destratification in China." Pp. 84-120 in *Class and Social Stratification in Post-Revolution China* (ed.) James L. Watson. Cambridge: Cambridge University Press.

Parish, William L. and Martin King Whyte. 1978. *Village and Family Life in Contemporary China*. Chicago: University of Chicago Press.

Pearson, Margaret M. 1997. *China's New Business Elite* (Berkeley: University of California Press.

Pepper, Suzanne. 1978. *Civil War in China: The Political Struggle, 1945-49*. Berkeley: University of California Press.

Pepper, Suzanne. 1996. *Radicalism and Education in 20th-Century China*. New York: Cambridge University Press.

Perkin, Frank. 1971. *Class Inequality & Political Order*. New York: Praeger.

Perry, Elizabeth J. and Li Xun. (eds.) 1997. *Proletarian Power: Shanghai in the Cultural Revolution*. Boulder: Westview Press.

Potter, Sulamith. 1983. "The Position of Peasants in Modern China's Social Order." 9/4: Pp. 465-499.

Potter, Sulamith and Jack M. Potter. 1990. *China's Peasants* (Cambridge and New York: Cambridge University Press.

Pye, Lucian. W. and Sidney Verba. (eds.) 1965. *Political Culture and Political Development*. Princeton: Princeton University Press.

Pye, Lucian. 1981. *The Spirit of Chinese Politics*. Cambridge: Oelgeschlager, Gunn & Hain.

Pye, Lucian. 1985. *Asian Power and Politics*. Cambridge: The Belnap Press.

Pye, Lucian. 1988. *The Mandarin and the Cadre*. Ann Arbor: Center for Chinese Studies, University of Michigan.

Pye, Lucian. 1990. "Tiananmen and Chinese Political Culture: The Escalation of Confrontation." Pp. 162-179 in *The Broken Mirror* (ed.) George Hicks. Chicago: St. James Press.

Quah, Stella R. et al. 1991. *Social Class in Singapore*. Centre for Advanced Studies, National University of Singapore: Times Academic Press.

Radock, David. 1977. *Political Behavior of Adolescents in China*. Tucson: The University of Arizona Press.

Rawski, Thomas G. 1989. *Economic Growth in Prewar China*. Berkeley: University of California Press.

Razman, Gilbert. 1973. *Urban Network in Ch'ing China and Tokugawa Japan*. Princeton: Princeton University Press.

Rehberg, C. Richard, Walder Schafer and Judie Sinclair. 1970. "Adolescent Achievement Behavior, Family Authority Structure, and Parental Socialization Practices." *American Journal of Sociology* 75: Pp. 1012-1034.

Rigby, Thomas Henry. 1979. "The Need for Comparative Research on Clientelism." *Studies in Comparative Communism* (Summer/Autumn) 12: Pp. 204-211.

Rigby, Thomas Henry. 1983. *Leadership Selection and Patron-Client Relations in the USSR and Yugoslavia.* London: Allen & Unwind.

Rosenberg, Morris. 1972. *Society and the Adolescent Self-Image.* Princeton: Princeton University Press.

Rosen, Stanley. 1982. *Red Guard Factionalism and the Cultural Revolution in Guangzhou.* Boulder: Westview Press.

Rosen, Stanley. 1990. "The Impact of Reform Policies on Youth Attitudes." Pp. 283-305 in *Chinese Society on the Eve of Tianamen* (eds.) Deborah Davis and Ezra Vogel. Cambridge: The Council on East Asian Studies, Harvard University.

Saari, John. 1977. *Legacies of Childhood.* San Francisco: Jossey-Bass Publishers.

Scalapino, Robert. 1972. "The Transition in Chinese Party Leadership." Pp. 67-148 in *Elites in the People's Republic of China* (ed.) Robert Scalapino. Seattle: University of Washington Press.

Scalapino, Robert. (ed.) 1972. *Elites in the People's Republic of China.* Seattle: University of Washington Press.

Scharm, Stuart R. (ed.) 1985. *The Scope of State Power in China.* London: School of Oriental and African Studies, University of London.

Schoenhals, Michael. (ed.) 1996. *China's Cultural Revolution 1966-1969.* Armonk: M. E. Sharpe.

Seybolt, Peter. 1977. *The Rustication of Urban Youth in China.* New York: M. E. Sharpe.

Seymour, James. 1980. *The Fifth Modernization.* New York: Human Rights Publishing Groups.

Sharma, K. L. 1986. *Caste, Class, and Social Movements.* Jaipur: Rawat Publications.

Shirk, Susan. 1982. *Competitive Comrades.* Berkeley: University of California Press.

Siu, Helen. 1989. *Agents and Victims in South China.* New Haven: Yale University Press.

Siu, Helen and Zelda Stern. (eds.) 1983. *Mao's Harvest.* New York: Oxford University Press.

Shue, Vivienne. 1980. *Peasant China in Transition.* Berkeley: University of California Press.

Solomon, Richard. 1972. *Mao's Revolution and the Chinese Political Culture.* Berkeley: University of California Press.

Srivastava, Anil K. 1986. *Social Class and Family Life in India.* Allahabad: Chugn Publication.

Statistical Bureau of Industry, Transportation, and Goods, People's Republic of China. 1985. *Zhongguo Gongye Jingji Tongji Ziliao 1949-1984* (Statistical Data of China's Industrial Economy, 1949-1984.). Beijing: China Statistical Publishing House.

State Personnel Bureau, People's Republic of China. 1986. *Renshi Gongzuo Wenjian Xuanbian, Vol. II* (A Selection of Documents on Personnel Management in China, Vol. II) (Beijing: Laodong Renshi Chubanshe).

State Statistical Bureau, People's Republic of China. 1982. *Zhongguo Tongji Nianjian 1981.* (China Statistical Yearbook 1981). Hong Kong: Jingji Daobaoshe.

State Statistical Bureau, People's Republic of China. *1983. Zhongguo Tongji Nianjian 1983.* (China Statistical Yearbook 1983). Hong Kong: Jingji Daobaoshe.

State Statistical Bureau, People's Republic of China. 1989. *Fenjin de Sishinian, 1949-1989.* (Forty Years of Progresses, 1949-1989). Beijing: China Statistical Publishing House.

State Statistical Bureau, People's Republic of China. 1998. *China Statistical Yearbook 1998.* Beijing: China Statistical Publishing House.

Su, Ji and Jia Lusheng. 1992. *Bai Mao Hei Mao, Zhongguo Gaige Xianzhuang Toushi* (White Cats and Black Cats, The Current Situations of China's Economic Reform). Changsha: Hunan Renmin Chubanshe.

Su, Xin. 1987. *Woguo Chengshi de Zhufang Wenti* (Urban Housing Problems in Our Country). Beijing: China Social Sciences Press.

Tapper, Ted. 1976. *Political Education and Stability.* London: John Wiley.

Teiwes, Frederick C. and Warren Sun. (eds.) 1993. *The Politics of Agricultural Cooperativization in China.* Armonk: M. E. Sharpe.

The General Trade Union of China. 1986. *Zhongguo Zhigong Duiwu Zhuangkuang Diaocha* (The Status of the Labor Force in Industry). Beijing: Gongren Chubanshe.

Thomas, William I. and Florian Znaniecki. 1984. *The Polish Peasant in Europe and America (1918-20).* Urbana: University of Illinois Press.

Thompson, E. P. 1966. *The Making of the English Working Class.* New York: Vintage Books.

Thurtson, Anne F. 1984/1985. "Victims of China's Cultural Revolution." Part 1, *Pacific Affairs* (Winter) 57: Pp. 599-620.

Thurtson, Anne F. 1985. "Victims of China's Cultural Revolution." Part 2, *Pacific Affairs* (Spring) 58: Pp. 5-27.

Thurston, Anne F. 1987. *Enemies of the People.* New York: Knopf.

Thurtson, Anne F. 1990. "Urban Violence During the Cultural Revolution." Pp. 149-174 in *Violence in China* (eds.) Jonathan Lipman and Steven Harrell. Albany: State University of New York Press.

Townsend, James. 1967. *The Revolutionization of Chinese Youth.* Berkeley: Center for Chinese Studies.

Treiman, Donald. 1977. *Occupational Prestige in Comparative Perspective.* New York: Academic Press.

Unger, Jonathan. 1982. *Education under Mao.* New York: Columbia University Press.

Unger, Jonathan. 1984. "The Class System in Rural China." Pp. 121-141 in *Class and Social Stratification in Post-Revolution* China (ed.) James L. Watson. Cambridge: Cambridge University Press.

Vaughan, Elizabeth. 1949. *Community under Stress.* Princeton: Princeton University Press.

Verba, Sidney and Norman Nie. 1972. *Participation in America.* New York: Harper & Row.

Walder, Andrew. 1986. *Communist Neo-Traditionalism.* Berkeley: University of California Press.

Walder, Andrew. 1987. "Wage Reform and the Web of Factory Interest." *The China Quarterly* (December) no. 109: Pp. 22-41.

Walder, Andrew. 1990. "Economic Reform and Income Distribution in Tianjin, 1976-1986." Pp. 135-156 in *Chinese Society on the Eve of Tianamen* (eds.) Deborah Davis and Ezra Vogel. Cambridge: The Council on East Asian Studies, Harvard University.

Walder, Andrew. 1992. "Property Rights and Stratification in Socialist Redistributive Economies." *American Sociological Review* 57/4: Pp. 524-539.

Walder, Andrew. 1995. "Career Mobility and the Communist Political Order." *American Sociological Review* 60/3: Pp. 309-328.

Waller, Derek. 1972. "The Evolution of the Chinese Communist Political Elites, 1931-1956." Pp. 41-66 in *Elites in the People's Republic of China* (ed.) Robert Scalapino. Seattle: University of Washington Press.

Wang, Kezhong et. al. 1987. *Dangdai Zhongguo de Zhigong Gongzi Fuli he Shehui Baoxian* (Wages, Benefits, and Social Security of State Workers in Contemporary China). Beijing: Zhongguo Shehui Kexue Chubanshe.

Wang, Shaoguang. 1995. *Failure of Charisma: The Cultural Revolution in Wuhan.* Hong Kong: Oxford University Press.

Wang, Yichu. 1960. "Western Impact and Social Mobility in China." *American Sociological Review* 25: Pp. 843-855.

Wank, David L. 1999. *Commodifying Communism.* Cambridge: Cambridge University Press.

Wasserstrom, Jeffery and Elizabeth Perry. (eds.) 1992. *Popular Protest and Political Culture in Modern China.* Boulder: Westview Press.

Watson, James L. (ed.) 1984. *Class and Social Stratification in Post-Revolution China.* Cambridge: Cambridge University Press.

White, Gordon. 1974. *The Politics of Class and Class Origins.* Canberra: Contemporary China Centre, The Australian National University.

White, Lynn. 1989. *Politics of Chaos.* Princeton: Princeton University Press.

White, Lynn. 1989. "A Leadership Diversifies." Pp. 67-113 in *Chinese Politics from Mao to Deng* (ed.) Victor Falkenheim. New York: Paragon House.

Whyte, Martin King. 1974. *Small Groups and Political Rituals in China.* Berkeley: University of California Press.

Whyte, Martin King. 1984. "Sexual Inequality under Socialism." Pp. 198-238 in *Class and Social Stratification in Post-Revolution China* (ed.) James L. Watson. Cambridge: Cambridge University Press.

Whyte, Martin King. 1986. "Social Trends in China." Pp. 103-123 in *Modernizing China* (eds.) A. Doak Barnett and Ralph N. Clough. Boulder: Westview Press.

Whyte, Martin King and William L. Parish. 1984. *Urban Life in Contemporary China.* Chicago: University of Chicago Press.

Whyte, William Foote. 1955. *Street Corner Society.* Chicago: University of Chicago Press.

Willerton, John. 1979. "Clientelism in the Soviet Union." *Studies in Comparative Communism* (Summer/Autume) 12: Pp. 159-211.

Wong, John. 1973. *Land Reform in the People's Republic of China.* New York: Praeger.

Xie, Yu and Emily Hannum. 1996. "Regional Variation in Earning Inequality in Reform-Era Urban China." *American Journal of Sociology* 101/4: Pp. 950-992.

Xue, Muqiao. 1981. *China's Socialist Economy.* Beijing: Foreign Languages Press.

Yan, Yunxiang, *The Flow of Gifts* (Stanford: Stanford University Press, 1996).

Yang, Dali L. 1996. *Calamity and Reform in China.* Stanford: Stanford University Press.

Yang, Jisheng. 1996. *"Touguo Cunzhe Kan Zhongguo."* (Relying on Saving Accounts to Understand China.), *Zhongguo Qingnian*, no. 10: Pp. 60-62.

Yang, Mayfair Mei-hui. 1994. *Gifts, Favors, and Banquets.* Ithaca: Cornell University Press.

Yang, Yiyong. 1999. *"Dangqian Zhongguo Jiuye Xingshi Fenxi."* (An Analysis of the Labor Market in China.), *Zhongguo Qingnian*, no. 8: Pp 9-10.

Yanowitch, Myrry and Wesley Fisher. (eds.) 1973. *Social Stratification and Mobility in the USSR.* White Plains, NY: International Arts and Sciences Press.

Yao, Shuben. 1986. *Sanshiwunian Zhigonggongzi Fazhan Gaishu* (An Outline of the Development of the Wage System in China for the Past 35 Years). Beijing: Laodong Renshi Chubanshe.

Yen, Chia-chi and Kao Kao. 1988. *The Ten-Year History of the Chinese Cultural Revolution.* Taiwan: Institute of Current China Studies.

Zang, Xiaowei. 1992. *Children of the Cultural Revolution: Class and Caste in Mao's China* (Ph.D. dissertation, University of California, Berkeley).

Zang, Xiaowei. 1995. "Industrial Management Systems and Managerial Ideologies in China*." Journal of Northeast Asian Studies* 14/1: Pp. 80-104

Zhang, Xin-Xiang and Wang Han-Sheng. 1992. "China: Stratification in Transition." paper presented at the annual meeting of the American Sociological Association.

Zhang, Zhenglong. 1989. *Xuebai Xuehong.* Beijing: PLA Publishing House.

Zhen, Yefu. 1985. *"Woguo Naoti Shouru Chabie De Lishi Bianqian Jiqi Fanxing"* (Reflections on the Historical Development of the Unfair Distribution of Income between Mental and Manual Workers in Our Country). *Shijie Jingji Daobao* (May) 9: p. 15.

Zhongguo Jiaoyu Nianjian Bianjibu. 1984. *Zhongguo Jiaoyu Nianjian, 1949-1981* (Yearbook of China's Education, 1949-1981). Beijing: China Encyclopedia Press.

Zhonggong Zhongyang Mao Zedong Xuanji Chuban Weiyuanhui (The Committee on Selected Works of Mao Zedong of the Central Committee of the Chinese Communist Party. 1969. *Mao Zedong Xuanji Vol. 1* (Selected Works of Mao Zedong Vol. 1). Beijing: Renmin Chubanshe.

Zhou, Xueguang and Liren Hou. 1999. "Children of the Cultural Revolution: The State and the Life Course in the People's Republic of China." *American Sociological Review* (1999) 64/1: Pp. 12-36.

Zhou, Xueguang, Nancy Brandon Tuma, and Phyllis Moen. 1997. "Institutional Change and Job-Shift Patterns in Urban China, 1949 to 1994." *American Sociological Review* 62/3: Pp. 393-365.

Index